C000132759

Queer Notions

A FABULOUS COLLECTION OF GAY AND LESBIAN WIT AND WISDOM

COMPILED BY DAVID BLANTON

RUNNING PRESS
PHILADELPHIA • LONDON

OTHER BOOKS IN THIS SERIES:

"But I Wouldn't Want to Live There!"
Edited by Michael Cader and Lisa Cader

Gardens
Compiled by Holly Hughes

Lawyer's Wit and Wisdom
Edited by Bruce Nash and Allan Zullo
Compiled by Kathryn Zullo

The Little Book of Phobias
Compiled by Joe Kohut

Medical Wit and Wisdom
Compiled by Jess M. Brallier

Meditations on the Earth
Compiled by Holly Hughes

The Quotable Cat
Compiled by C. E. Crimmins

The Quotable Woman

The Wit and Wisdom of Women

9 8 7 6 5 4 3 2 1
Digit on the right indicates the number of this printing.

Library of Congress Cataloging-in-Publication Number
95–70147

ISBN 1–56138–684–7

Cover and interior design by Paul Kepple
Edited by Brian Perrin

Front cover illustrations by Jerry Jankowski. Reproduced or created from *Mostly Happy Clip Art*, Volumes 1 and 2.

Back cover illustrations: Top left and top right © CSA Archives. Bottom left and bottom right by Jerry Jankowski. Reproduced or created from *Mostly Happy Clip Art*, Volumes 1 and 2.

Interior illustrations (except pp. 92, 177, 208) by Jerry Jankowski. Reproduced or created from *Mostly Happy Clip Art*, Volumes 1 and 2.

This book may be ordered by mail from the publisher.
Please add $2.50 for postage and handling.

But try your bookstore first!
Running Press Book Publishers
125 South Twenty-second Street
Philadelphia, Pennsylvania 19103–4399

DEDICATION

For James and Bob.

I miss you girls. I promised you my first born: here she is.

Special thanks to Gregg Stebben and Adam Ducker.

CONTENTS

When my agent, Jennifer, first presented this project to me, I was skeptical, to say the least. *Does the world really need a gay quote book?* I didn't think so at the time, but, for reasons I no longer recall, I agreed to do it.

I'm so glad I did. In the months that followed, I delved into a world that I thought I knew. *I searched through every medium I could think of*—literature, film, theater, comedy, the press, television—gay, lesbian, bisexual, transgendered, and yes, even straight. *What I found was astounding.*

Breadth, depth, wisdom, pathos—all of these, of course, I found in abundance. And, in a community that prides itself on a well-turned phrase, there was no lack of wit, subtlety, arched eyebrow, and irony. But, beyond that, I discovered the degree to which our existence—despite the official line—resonates in the larger world.

You wouldn't know it at a casual glance, but the straight world and the mass media know *we're more than the stereotypes sometimes used to represent us.* We do have friends—people who love us, people who like us, people who are just plain decent. We also have enemies—you know who they are, and you'll find their voices in this collection, too.

We all know the pain of homophobia, the tragedy of AIDS, the fear of discrimination—the things that can make us feel disenfranchised and marginal. *But we must also remember the joy of love,* the ecstasy of sex, the comforts of friendship and family, and the thrill of the struggle for justice. I've tried to incorporate all of these things here.

This book was a beautiful journey for me. I hope it will be the same for you.

DEFINING OURSELVES

ho • mo • sex • u • al (hō-mə-'seksh-(ə)wel, -mō-) adj.
of, relating to, or having a sexual orientation to persons of the
same sex   n. a homosexual person; a gay man or lesbian

Everyone is born naked and after that, everything is drag.

RU PAUL

You have to do what comes naturally. Can you imagine a plum tree refusing to grow plums? When you repress yourself, that's what you're attempting to do.

NANCY ANDERSON

I think I've been gay since I was a fetus.

KEVIN ELYOT

All my life I've loved women, and that's it. I've never been any other way.

LINDA PERRY

We're here, we're queer. It's a natural thing.

ROMANOVSKY AND PHILIPS

I ascertain that I am homosexual. Okay that's no cause for alarm. How and why are idle questions. It's a little like wanting to know why my eyes are green.

JEAN GENET

Queer
Notions
page 12

The fact that I'm gay isn't going to make a diddly-squat's worth
of difference. I won't let it.

JACK BAKER

I like the word gay, though I think of myself more
as queer. I believe the strength in my work comes
from that perspective—my being an outsider.

HOLLY HUGHES

I am grateful to be gay because I belong to a people who have right on their side,
and I know that justice is on the way.

ARNIE KANTROWITZ

*We don't live in a lavender bubble.
We live in the world.*

URVASHI VAID

Being queer is like being on a lifetime assignment as a
secret agent in some foreign country.

NORETTA KOERTGE

Gay culture is far from "marginal," being rather "intersectional,"
the conduit between unlike beings.

JUDY GRAHN

**For those of you with alternative lifestyles, in England
it's alright to be a queen.**

ANONYMOUS

**The universe is not only queerer than we imagine,
but it is queerer that we can imagine.**

J. B. S. HALDANE

We have made ourselves up, in short, like all the other Americans, determined
to establish their own cultural identity. But also like all those other lonely,
immigrant Americans, we are addicted to the ideology of continual self-reinvention.

FRANK BROWNING

*Our culture is the manifest
content of our lives, not a carefully
constructed recruiting brochure.*

TONY KUSHNER

The world is damn queer—it really is.
But people won't recognize
the immensity of its queerness.

Lytton Strachey

I don't wish us to be ghettoized. I don't wish it to be impossible for us
to be accepted for whom we wish to be accepted.

EDWARD ALBEE

There aren't two worlds. A gay world with a small "w" and then the World
with a capital "W"; there is only the World, and it is seen from
our world, seen from—and imagined from—our culture.

NEIL BARTLETT

**This boy liked the gay life—the clothes, the way people talked
and walked and held themselves—but if you can believe it,
he didn't realize there was more to being gay than that!**

DICK ADDISON

Putting a label [homosexual] on myself was a big step forward . . .
once I said, "Yes, that's me, that's what I am," I was able to work with it.

BARBARA GITTINGS

Are you a Lesbian? Everything pauses, faces look up in terrible silence.
I hear them not breathe. That word in public, the word I waited
half a lifetime to hear. Finally I am accused.

KATE MILLETT

After Stonewall we were fighting for the right to behave
homosexually, to commit homosexual acts. Now the goal has shifted;
we are arguing for the right to *identify* as homosexuals.

MICHAEL BRONSKI

*I know you've heard all the rumors.
And, yes, it's true. I'm a le…, le…,
Lawrence Welk fan.*

K. D. LANG

**Visibility is important, psychologically,
because of the profound role played by its
opposite in the life of every homosexual
that is, secretiveness.**

PAUL ROBINSON

I don't want to be labeled as either a pansy or a heterosexual.
Labeling is so self-limiting. We are what we do—not what we say we are.

MONTGOMERY CLIFF

Labels are for filing, labels are for clothing, labels are not for people.

Martina Navratilova

This question is so direct—are you gay or not? If somebody excites me, either a man or a woman, then I'm interested.

UDO KIER

I don't need to join a club in order to go to bed with a man.

JAMES BALDWIN

I've been with women for fourteen years, and I've been with a man for two. I'm still a dyke. The homosexual part of me never goes away.

MARIA MAGGENTI

If I'm making love to a woman that I love, I wouldn't necessarily be a lesbian just because she might call herself that. I feel my sexuality is as individual as my soul, and it keeps getting enriched.

SOPHIE B. HAWKINS

I like to be able to think for myself. I think we get so stuck on definitions and types. I know a lot of people type themselves. I've been around people where the defining element of their life is being gay. I can see good and bad in any extreme.

DAN BUTLER

. . . a lot of people just thought I was 100 percent homosexual. That's not really the case. Nor am I 100 percent heterosexual. Nor do I adhere to or appreciate the label bisexual. I think it's kind of cheap. It's confining. It's putting a male geometric set of rules onto something that I think of as female and very fluid. . . .

MICHAEL STIPE

When I first started dating women there was this pressure to define myself, to say, "I am a lesbian." That was another generation talking. Even if I end up settled down with this woman, how can I say I'm a lesbian if I'm capable of loving a man?

ANJI DICKSON

I think most people know now that I'm in a relationship with a man. There were people who were angry about it and felt betrayed. You know I'm still here and I'm still very much involved in lesbian culture and supporting lesbian and gay rights. I cannot disconnect myself from my feelings about the gay and lesbian community and that part of myself which is a lesbian.

HOLLY NEAR

I guess I'm bisexual. Or maybe when I quit smoking I just needed something to put in my mouth.

STEPHANIE SMITH

I know I'm not a man . . . and I've come to the conclusion that I'm probably not a woman either. The trouble is, we're living in a world that insists we be one or the other.

KATE BORNSTEIN

It is easy to backslide into the popular but untenable position of artificially dividing all people into heterosexual and homosexual categories, and thinking of them as normal versus abnormal. To the unwary this supports the unsupportable notion that maleness comes in two varieties: regular and impaired, and if you are on the bottom you always are.

C. A. TRIPP

I am personally sick of liberals who say they don't care who sleeps with whom, it's what you do outside of bed that counts. This is what homosexuals have been trying to get straights to understand for years.

MARTHA SHELLEY

*Except for our choice of love, life,
and sex partner we are really just like
any other people in society.*

DEL MARTIN

Gays have nothing in common with straight people except what we do in bed.

RICHARD GOLDSTEIN

Because of our situation, God has given us an opportunity to almost transcend
our gender, which gives us a vision and sensitivity that other people don't have. They think
that being white and male is going to save the world; but life is not *The Lion King*.

JASON REEVES

Homosexual men and women, in fact, have been crucial to [the] process of shaping more humane ideals of the masculine and the feminine.

JAMES CARROLL

In these days of lesbian chic, the walls surrounding our flourishing community seem
unusually permeable. Excited postadolescent women with flushed cheeks
flow in and out of our collective warm embrace . . . reading Vita Sackville-West
by day and *On Our Backs* when the sun goes down.

MERYL COHN

*Everyone wants to be a dyke now;
everyone craves our freedom, guts,
and knowing looks.*

SUSIE BRIGHT

We're like the Evian water of the '90s. Everyone wants to know a lesbian or
to be with a lesbian or just to dress like one.

SUZANNE WESTENHOEFER

When I hang out with my gay women friends I say, "Damn, they look happy. I wonder if I've made the right choice?"

ANONYMOUS

DEFINING
OURSELVES
page 23

Well, the last time I checked I was 100% lezbo.
No penis envy here.

MONICA PALACIOS

Yes I am.

MELISSA ETHERIDGE

I am not a straight girl; I am a femme. There's a huge difference, even though
it may not be obvious to the untrained heart or eye.

RAPHAELLA VAISSEAU

*I __am__ a dyke, __that's__ why
I look like one.*

DANA ROSE

I call myself a born-again butch. Which means I still have the
choreography but I don't do the dance.

ROBIN TYLER

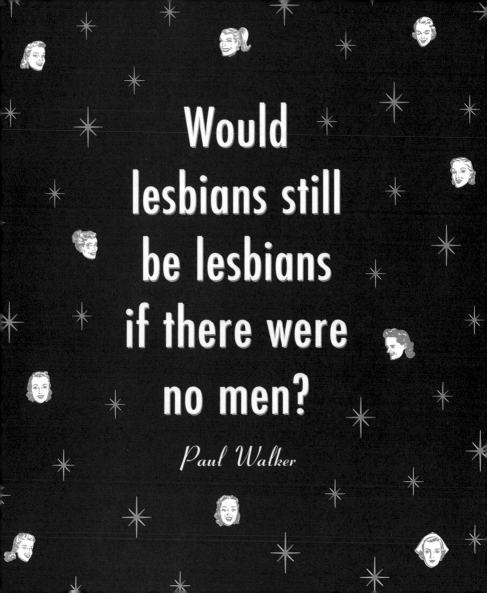

I posit my own freedom. I place myself with all who will be
women no longer: lesbians.

JENNIFER ALLEN

Lesbianism represents a commitment of skin, blood, breast, and bone.

CATHERINE R. STIMPSON

A lesbian is the rage of all women condensed to the point of explosion.

RADICALESBIANS

Didn't you always want Wonder Woman to be a dyke?

STEPHANIE MADYUN

Lesbians and other oppressed people have a bigger
burden to bear because the rest of the world spends a lot of
time telling us we should feel bad about ourselves.

NANCY LANOUE

It's one thing to be a lesbian;
it's another thing to be a bulldyke.

CYNTHIA TORELLI

It's a bitch being butch.

LESLEA NEWMAN

There is nothing mixed up about a woman who loves women, who wants to
have sex with them, or who identifies as a lesbian. It is society that is mixed up
because it punishes people for not conforming to its gender stereotypes.

EDWARD STEIN

The lesbian, however hated or oppressed,
is the purest representation of the liberated ideal.

JILL JOHNSTON

Ironically groups of nuns or lesbians are often mistaken for one another today,
since we often travel in female packs oblivious to male attention or needs.

ROSEMARY CURB

**DEFINING
OURSELVES**
page 27

A minority is only thought of as a minority when it constitutes some kind of threat to the majority, real or imaginary. And no threat is ever *quite* imaginary.

CHRISTOPHER ISHERWOOD

Outsiders develop humor as a defense; why do you think most comedians are gay or Jewish?

PAUL LYNDE

Of course it is extremely difficult to like oneself in a culture which thinks you are a disease.

CHRYSTOS

Also, what was the difference whether you have the stigma of being a homosexual or the stigma of being a promiscuous homosexual? If you're going to be stigmatized, the least you can do is enjoy it.

JOHN REID

Straight society is really down on blatant gays, and that affects and oppresses all gay people, because gays won't be treated as beautiful human beings until even the most "flaming faggots" and "diesel dykes" are respected in our community, as well as in straight society.

BRIAN CHAVEZ

I know I can't tell you what it is to be gay.
But I can tell you what it's not.
It's not hiding behind words, Mama. Like family
and decency and Christianity.

ARMISTEAD MAUPIN

. . . gay people are smarter. If you weren't smart you wouldn't figure out what
it was. You'd probably grow up, get married and just think that you liked
your buddies a lot and that your wife was a lousy lay.

ERIC TOWNES

When I was 13 years old there were only two things I knew about lesbians:
they wore green on Thursdays and had hairy nipples.

DOROTHY ALLISON

*I had my first wide-awake orgasm
while staring at a magazine photograph
of the Yale swimming team.*

RICHARD AMORY

I resent like hell that I was maybe eighteen
years old before I even heard the L-word.

MICHELLE SHOCKED

My father took me for a walk up a lane. . . . He said: ". . . Do you know
what buggers are? Buggers are two men who work themselves up into such a state
of mutual admiration that one puts his piss-pipe up the other one's arse.
What do you think of that?"

JOHN BETJEMAN

This was a time and place where the notion of growing up gay
was simply unimaginable, not because it seemed bad or sick in the way
that homosexuals were seen to be bad, sick people, but because there
was at large no idea or model of what a gay life might be.

FRANK BROWNING

My struggle has allowed me to transcend that sense of shame
and stigma identified with my being a Black gay man. Having come
through the fire, they can't touch me.

MARLON RIGGS

**DEFINING
OURSELVES**
page 31

Homophobia is easier for black people where black people are concerned.
They feel they have the right to correct me on my behavior. There is this notion
that homosexuality is something that white people do.

DAVID MCALMONT

I think being a Jew makes you an outsider; just like being queer makes you an outsider.
Actually, growing up a Jew was good training for becoming a Lesbian.

LESLEA NEWMAN

Just because I like to suck cock doesn't make me any less American than Jesse Helms.

ALLEN GINSBURG

As a fag, I make an effort to present a much wider persona than just a guy who dresses like a girl.

D—L ALVAREZ

I don't want to become an identity junky.

JAN CLAUSSEN

*Queer Notions*
page 32

We [bisexuals] are tired of being analyzed, defined and represented
by people other than ourselves or worse yet, not considered at all. We are frustrated
by the imposed isolation and invisibility that comes from being told or expected
to choose either a homosexual or heterosexual identity.

ANYTHING THAT MOVES MAGAZINE

I used to think it was terrible to be black. . . .
Now I think it is more terrible to be gay.
Nobody ever treated me as bad for being black
as I got treated for being a dyke.

TERRY OSBORN

A black homosexual is somebody who is in for a lot of problems.
If not because he's black, then because he's homosexual; then it's because
he's an extreme homosexual who makes no attempt to hide it.

WAYNE ALEXANDRE

When you're gay, I think that overrides being an interracial couple.
When we're together, I don't think people think,
"Oh they're an interracial couple." They think, "Oh, they're a gay couple."

JONATHAN VAN METER

I am a black man with a sexual preference for white men. It's really no different than preferring vodka to scotch, except that I'm often judged by it.

DARRYL TOWLES

I've been the bull's eye of criticism from African-American men who subscribe to the notion that I, like all black men, should exclusively pursue each other. Welcome to the real world, my brothers.

STEVEN CORBIN

What drag is really about is becoming more aware of the two genders within ourselves.

TERRENCE STAMP

Dressing up in drag was a natural thing. It just came together. I guess it was like a straight man becoming a police officer.

GIRLINA

You put on a dress and people treat you completely differently.
If I go to a club as a slim, rock n'roll fag, no one pays me any attention.
But put on a dress and everybody wants to talk to you.

MISTRESS FORMIKA

Every man should own at least one dress—and so should lesbians.

JANE ADAMS SPAHR

The world used to be a place where there were definite lines between those
who did drag and those who didn't. Now when I pass a construction site
and see some burly man with a pile driver gyrating in his callused hands, I have
to think to myself, "Does this man have a secret desire to be a Judy,
Liza, or Barbra impersonator?" When will it stop?

HEDDA LETTUCE

**Feeling sexy for the first time in my life, enjoying the catcalls.
I'm in drag and I'm faking them out.**

KIM KLAUSNER

I'm basically a homosexual man. I love clothes. I love good, fine fabrics. I work out. I'm concerned about my looks. I'm vain.

SARAH JESSICA PARKER

Sexual orientation is only one aspect of homosexuality, which is really a personality, a sensitivity, a spirit. . . . It is an inexorable part of what makes one an individual.

RICHARD FRIEDEL

The modern queer was invented by Tennessee Williams. Brando in blue jeans, sneakers, white T-shirt and leather jacket. When you saw that, you knew they were available.

DEREK JARMAN

Not all gays respond to the same stuff. Would Alexander the Great have loved *Auntie Mame*?

BRUCE BAWER

Gays don't want all the same things
at the same time. So it's no surprise that some of
us focus on maintaining cruising venues while
others fight for the right to marry.

STEPHEN MILLER

There's a self-conscious attempt in the gay movement to look like the black civil rights
movement and there is a superficial resemblance, but only a superficial one.

LEONARD GOLDSTEIN

I do not want to enter into the debate
of who has suffered more, trivializing the debate
by comparing levels of misery. There's enough
suffering to go around.

DAVID BERGMAN

If they want to play at politics, postmodern gays must decide whether to
sign on as a gender or an ethnicity. Unfortunately, neither model fits.

CALEB CRAIN

Identity politics is a dead-end pit where you can only plunge deeper into your terminal uniqueness.

PHILL WILSON

Separation is the great dictator of wrong decisions. When you live in your own universe, you're bound to get your shit shocked back into place.

RONNY GALICKI

I didn't choose to be black or to be born female,
however I'm quite proud and happy to be both.
I don't believe that people choose their sexual preference,
and they have every right to be proud and enjoy
their sexuality. You all may not think it's the same type
of thing, but from where I stand and
what I see discrimination and oppression feels and looks
just as ugly. Now, let's move on.

JULIA BOYD

You can be a straight white male in a pin-stripe suit and still have more pain than a black lesbian single mother. And that's the truth of life. People aren't willing to look beyond the masks.

SCOTT THOMPSON

CHAPTER TWO

BEYOND
the
CLOSET

"Look out world! Here I come!"

The single most important thing you can do politically for gay rights is to come out. Not to write a letter to your congressman but to come out.

BARNEY FRANK

Every gay person must come out. . . .
Once they realize we are indeed their children, we are
indeed everywhere, every myth, every lie, every innuendo
will be destroyed once and for all.

HARVEY MILK

*Once homosexuality comes out
into the open, it's very
hard to frame it as something
horrible or unnatural.*

RICHARD D. MOHR

Being honest about one's sexuality helps to turn ignorance into acceptance.

AMANDA BEARSE

Queer
Notions

Honesty is usually grounds for rejection.

KIKI MASON

It is better to be hated for what one is than to be loved for what one is not.

ANDRÉ GIDE

If you want to look like the people next door, you're probably smothering yourself and your dreams.

CLIVE BARKER

Whoever expects acceptance doesn't want to be known.

MICHAEL KLEIN

*I was hiding in fear
of being found out—by myself.*

HARRY CLEIN

There are as many rationalizations for
staying closeted as there are gay men and lesbians.

URVASHI VAID

The closet people, we who know about the safety of
closets, we are safe and comfortable, but until all your people
have justice, you can't have justice yourself.

MEL WHITE

Coming out is not a one-day event but an ongoing process
and should begin not when a subculture-designated calendar says it should,
but when the individual is prepared to face the consequences.

BRUCE BAWER

No matter how high-sounding the rhetoric, outing makes some of the most
august gay journalists and leaders look like a lot of bitchy queens
on the set of *Boys in the Band*, bent not on helping each other but on
clawing each other. It's not a pretty sight.

RANDY SHILTS

Why is being outed such a big deal?
When I find out that someone's gay, my respect
for them increases tenfold.

SCOTT THOMPSON

I've been outed and I'm not even in.

JERRY SEINFELD

I consider truthful discussion of the lives of homosexual public figures
as legitimate and significant in the larger aim to give courage to millions
of gay people who stay in the closet out of fear and shame.

MICHELANGELO SIGNORILE

Saying someone is gay who is gay no longer constitutes defamation or slander or libel. You cannot defame someone by telling the truth.

LARRY KRAMER

You come out when you're ready, just like everything else
in this world. You can't do it if you're not ready to face your family
and friends, your co-workers or the world. . . .

JUAN PALOMO

**BEYOND
THE CLOSET**
page 45

There are those who see being gay or lesbian as tragic, coming out as a nightmarish ordeal, a gauntlet that we must run in order to experience the even more painful process of learning not to hate ourselves, to accept who we are. While there are those who have good reason to feel that way, I strongly suspect that a lot more of us don't.

BOB SATULOFF

There is no torment in coming out. The torment is in being in.

ARMISTEAD MAUPIN

Nothing has happened to me out of the closet that was anywhere near as dangerous as being closeted.

KAREN THOMPSON

In the fall of 1931, I decided on the basis of not a great deal of information and not too much experience that I didn't want to live the life of a lie, so I declared myself on campus to all the people that I knew . . . most of the people I knew did stay away, but the people I loved the best said, "Okay, what else is new?"

HENRY HAY

I would just drink myself to sleep and then wake up and get ready for the next game. There is no way I could continue to play and stay closeted. I was being paid to concentrate on baseball, but staying in the closet takes as much concentration as playing.

STEVE MATHIS

I read where an athlete recently came out and said he was gay.
So what? I know 50,000 athletes who are queer as a bat.

JOHNNY MATHIS

Revealing my sexuality changed me as a person, it changed my self-confidence, and my attitude toward the world. It's released in me an anger and a passion to get laws changed. . . . [and] I am a better actor.

IAN MCKELLEN

The closet symbolizes isolation, the individual without society, a stranger even to the self.

KATHY WESTON

When, at the age of twenty-one, I walked into my first gay bar (The 1270 on Boylston Street in Boston) it was like walking through the looking glass for the first time to the right side . . . I knew the sheer joy of seeing women dancing with women and men with men, understanding for the first time why anyone would want to dance with anyone.

NANCY L. WILSON

Let's come out and dispel the rumors and lies that are being spread about us. Let's come out and set everybody straight, so to speak.

MARTINA NAVRATILOVA

I finally said to the editor-in-chief, "I'm a lesbian. Please stop it. I don't want to meet your brother-in-law. . . ." It was so much fun the next Monday I went to all of the editors' offices and came out.

LINDA VILLAROSAS

The Lord is my shepherd and He knows I'm gay.

TROY PERRY

By staying closeted we make ourselves invisible; by coming out we shatter
the popular illusion that the whole world is heterosexual.

ROMANOVSKY AND PHILLIPS

How sick I am of keeping a mask on my countenance. How tight it sticks it makes me sore.

WILLIAM BECKFORD

The walls of the closet are guarded by the dogs of terror, and inside of
the closet is a house of mirrors.

JUDY GRAHN

We can easily forgive a child who is afraid of the dark;
the real tragedy of life is when adults are afraid of the light.

PLATO

*Being out means doing what
your grandmother told
you to do, which is not to lie.*

BARBARA SMITH

Queer
Notions

We spend vast amounts of our emotional energy learning how not to be
natural and in eluding the trap of our own nature.

JAMES BALDWIN

There are many lesbians and gay men trapped by their fear
into silence and invisibility, and they exist
in a dim valley of terror wearing nooses of conformity.

AUDRE LORDE

*Oppression can only survive
through silence.*

CARMEN DE MONTEFLORES

I wish that homosexuals were born with a
little horn in the middle of their foreheads so we
couldn't hide so easily. At least if you can't hide,
you have to stand up and fight.

HARVEY FIERSTEIN

The moment you can learn to deal with homosexuality in art,
it's quite an exciting moment, just as in a sense when people "come out"
it's quite an exciting moment. It means they become aware of their desires,
and can deal with them in a remarkably honest way.

DAVID HOCKNEY

I've always made a point of being open about my sexuality because I saw a generation of gay authors who were not and I was disgusted by their behavior.

ARMISTEAD MAUPIN

When I was young, I felt it was no good writing books about homosexuality,
because they were only ever read by other homosexuals,
and the same with plays and movies. Somebody had to live it. Somebody
had to be seen as a homosexual.

QUENTIN CRISP

I'd rather be serving time in a women's jail where there's at least sex, than being in the closet in Hollywood.

MARGA GOMEZ

On a spiritual level I believe that
confronting the fear of coming out loosened up
and freed all other aspects of my life.

MELISSA ETHERIDGE

My music is so damned honest, I think it would be really horrible not to be honest
with my fans. How can I be shut-mouthed about the fact that I'm gay?

MELISSA FERRICK

I never had any problems with being
a homosexual. I mean look at me. I was
always right out there.

TRUMAN CAPOTE

*I don't want to be involved
in some sort of scandal, but I've
covered the waterfront.*

TENNESSEE WILLIAMS

Things have changed. No more hiding, no more guilty
transgressive sex. But the habit of invisibility has been so strong that even
in coming out we have managed to hide ourselves.

LEO BERSANI

I have learned that coming out is a daily process,
not limited to where we live, who we're linked to, or how we
conduct our lives. It is understanding your place in the world,
born of your own family; it is entwined with your personal ideas
and the goals you set. Alas, these things are ever-changing,
and you have to keep discovering new ways to exist as a
gay or lesbian person while making your life whole.

TOM CURTICE

I say that it is time to open the closet door and let in the fresh air
and the sunshine; it is time to doff and discard the secrecy,
the disguise, and the camouflage; it is time to hold up your heads and to
look the world squarely in the eye as the homosexuals that you are,
confident in the knowledge that as objects of prejudice and victims of
discrimination you are right and they are wrong, and confident of the rightness
of what you are and of the goodness of what you do. Gay is good. It is.

FRANK KAMENY

Slowly but surely, gay people are coming around to the idea that if you continue to be invisible, that's all you will be, and it's not a nice life.

BEV CLARK

When I see young men and old women come out of the closet and face being called faggots and dykes and pariahs and betrayers of the family dream, then I am honored to be gay because I belong to a people who are proud.

ARNIE KANTROWITZ

There's a glorious, ecstatic feeling in being seen, in being out there, especially after so many years of hiding. This is me, come and take it.

SARA CYTRON

We must be proud of who we are, and we cannot do that when we hide.

MARTINA NAVRATILOVA

If a bullet should enter my brain, let that bullet destroy every closet door.

HARVEY MILK

CHAPTER THREE

The POLITICS *of* PRIDE

"If elected the first gay President, I promise there will finally be equal rights for all!"

If the Berlin Wall can come down, so can the wall keeping
gays and lesbians as outlaws.

PHYLLIS BURKE

*Mainstream America has to
realize we are everywhere; and then relax.*

W. SCOTT THOMPSON

Our struggle is the last great chapter in the long history of civil rights in this country.

GERRY STUDDS

We want something which is unique
among oppressed groups: the right to have the sex
we want without being punished for it.

LEO BERSANI

One lie has been the singularly most effective propaganda tool
against social equity: presenting us consistently as isolated and pathologized
neurotics who are special-interest while continuing to present heterosexual
white males as neutral, objective, and value-free.

SARAH SCHULMAN

Queer
Notions

Other people get money for being married;
they get health benefits for being married; they get money
for having children. When we want to be able to
kiss and hold hands on the street without being beat up,
suddenly we're asking for special rights.

MARK FISHER

The only "special right" that the United States government gives to minorities
is the right to be the target of genocidal policies. We have only to look
at AIDS policy to confirm this truth.

MAB SEGREST

I'm not willing to just be tolerated.
That wounds my love of love and of liberty.

JEAN COCTEAU

People can tolerate two homosexuals they see leaving together,
but the next day they're smiling, holding hands, tenderly embracing one another,
then they cannot be forgiven. It is not the departure for pleasure
that is unacceptable, it is waking up happy.

MICHEL FOUCAULT

Justice for gay men and lesbians will be advanced only when we are
accepted and supported in this society *despite* our differences from the dominant culture.

PAULA L. ETTELBRICK

By aspiring to join the mainstream rather than
figuring out the ways we need to change it, we risk loosing our
gay and lesbian souls in order to gain the world.

URVASHI VAID

*One of the problems with
so-called moderate gay and lesbian
Americans is that they believe
that they're citizens. They're not.*

MARK FISHER

Even the most progressive liberals insist on turning democracy itself into an
empty signifier that points to a better, more tolerant, and less homophobic future
only on condition that such a future be eternally delayed.

PETER MCLAREN

Today's conservatives have no role for homosexuals; they want them to disappear,
an option that was once illusory and is now impossible.

ANDREW SULLIVAN

*I wish this issue would just go away
but I know it can't.*

GEORGE BUSH, ON GAY RIGHTS

. . . I'll be out there letting people know I'm a "dyke" and fighting
homophobia by educating those who are ignorant.

A. JARRETT KING

The more we demand that institutions allow us to be who we are,
the more they're going to have to.

STEPHEN HERBITS

Our greatest challenge rests in finding
a language, a way of communicating across
our subjective, across difference.

MARLON RIGGS

The function of the queer press is not advocacy, but agitation.

MASHA GESSEN

The gay community has become so much more aggressive.
No one's going to take it anymore, the oppression and all the hate, for no reason.

BILL VAN PARYS

It was inevitable that outrageousness exploded with the beginnings of gay liberation. Hooray
for sassy risk and silly experiment and anarchic joy!

JAMES BROUGHTON

It's time we did something to assert ourselves.
After all, we do comprise 10% of the population.

ALLEN GINSBERG

Coming out to people who love and respect you is
the most important political act you can do.

TIM MCFEELEY

Coming out is no longer the sum total of our strategy; we are about power.

JOHN D'EMILIO

We have a right to be visible, we have a right to be safe. We have a right to build our own culture, our own institutions.

OUTLOOK MAGAZINE

The gay parade is a jubilant expression of pride. Its primary function is to make the enigmatic notion of community a tangible force that cannot be ignored.

NICOLE EISENMAN

The lesbian and gay movement grapples with issues of sexual diversity—bi and otherwise—because it's fully diverse itself, a microcosm of the larger society in which homosexuality is only the biggest of many secrets that refuse to stay silent.

CAROL A. QUEEN

If you can't raise consciousness, at least raise hell.

Rita Mae Brown

Like one big gay pride march, gay and lesbian politics
of recent years have heralded our sheer existence: "We're here,
we're queer, and we're not going shopping."

ARA WILSON

Dignity as an ideal, importantly, is something, unlike happiness, which gays can
achieve to a significant degree independently of the good will of the dominant culture:
it can be experienced in the very political procedures that gays choose.

RICHARD D. MOHR

*There are as many politics of
homosexuality as there are words for it.*

ANDREW SULLIVAN

I became an activist to reconcile myself, and to give voice to experiences
of oppression, and to resist the slow death of silence and inaction.

CARMEN VASQUEZ

It's tremendously empowering when you're gay to realize that you've been doing
it right, and it's the bigots who are stumbling about in a fog.

HOWARD CRUSE

**THE
POLITICS
OF PRIDE**
page 65

I was going to raise my gay consciousness but that turned out to be too much work.

JAMES TURCOTTE

Real love cannot be silent in the face of injustice.

MEL WHITE

Silence is not protection enough.

CHRISTOPHER ROBINSON

Sometimes you have to speak your mind rather than mind your speech.

ANONYMOUS

Socratic love prefers anarchy to slavery.

ROGER PEYREFRITTE

Gay is a process of attaining mutual and equal social and sexual relationships among all human beings, which is realized only through participation in the free dynamic expression of love among people of the same sex.

GAY LIBERATION FRONT MANIFESTO

Queer
Notions

Gay liberation is inherently revolutionary.

ANONYMOUS

Gay power is where you have a strong pride in your own minority, not quite arrogance, and where you feel there's no institution and no person on this earth that can take away your freedom or that has any right to tell you what to do as long as you don't interfere with the rights of others.

JIM OWLERS

I get very angry and frustrated with young gay guys who say they don't think or care about politics. They're the most vulnerable and disempowered group in American society and they don't care about politics. Can anything be more absurd than that?

MARK FISHER

You can't separate politics from life because the effects are constant.

JAMES EARL HARDY

I'm very militant, you know, in a quiet way.

CHRISTOPHER ISHERWOOD

I am by no means a stranger to gay militancy, and I have spoken
out sharply against the oppression of gays by straight society. Nevertheless,
even if society were changing radically today or tomorrow and gays would
suddenly find total acceptance, we would still have to deal with our pasts,
we would still have to come to terms with all those years we spent in real
inner and outer conflict. And it is my contention that in those conflicts
can be seen some unexpected but very real blessings.

EDMUND WHITE

Agitators are a set of interfering people, who come down to some perfectly contented class of the community and sow the seeds of discontent among them. That is the reason agitators are so absolutely necessary.

OSCAR WILDE

I'm sure that lipstick lesbians do have politics. Just don't tell them this;
they'll think I'm telling them to vote.

JEANNE CORDOVA

Lesbians not only politicize our differences,
but eroticize them as well. We just don't talk about it.

CARLA TRUJILLO

The movement should be called "lesbian connectionism," not "lesbian separatism."

ANN JAPENGA

I have a vision of a progressive, multiracial lesbian and gay diaspora that
includes and celebrates the stories and cultural discourse of all our people. It is a vision
that can become a reality only if we move beyond the rhetoric of the "isms" to action
and the creation of organizations that put an end to our isolating ways.

CARMEN VASQUEZ

*European gay-rights movements have
created a political culture
that Americans can only dream of.*

SHELLY ANDERSON

The term "liberal" used to mean that you liked Jews; now it means that you
like blacks; in the future maybe it'll mean you like gays.

LEONARD GOLDSTEIN

Queer
Notions
page 70

There are a lot of parallels between the ban on gay
marriage and the laws of the past that prohibited interracial
marriage. Basically, in both cases, it's two people trying to decide
what a family is to them and it's outside the law.

STEPHANIE SMITH

There is an ancient correlation not only of military service and homosexuality,
but of democracy in particular with military service on the part
of all citizens, which extends from ancient history to the present day. It is perhaps time
that one of the leading modern democracies in the world recognized it.

JOHN BOSWELL

The seeming lack of any willingness to understand the politics of gay and
lesbian liberation colludes with the dominant white male culture
to repressnot only gay men and lesbians, but also to repress a natural part of all
human beings, namely the bisexual potential in us all.

CHERYL CLARK

When people put down feminism and gay rights,
they always talk about "family" and "morality." That's bullshit;
what they're talking about is power.

LOWELL BEAN

Sometimes people fight intolerance in a rather intolerant manner.

PAUL CADMUS

I think we need to remember how easy it is to develop a fundamentalist
viewpoint while fighting fundamentalism.

ROBERT BATTEN

By drawing such a clearly bigoted line in the sand on lesbian and gay issues,
the right wing may have done us a favor in the long run.

TOM DUANE

I'm not going against God's will because I love a man;
you're going against God's will because you're trying to put out
my light and I can't allow that.

JASON REEVES

Use of the term heterosexism will tell the heterosexuals that it is their problem, not ours.

JOSEPH H. NEISEN

Do you want to protect your children from gay influence? Very well. Destroy the *Mona Lisa* and *The Last Supper*, silence *Messiah* and *Swan Lake*, and burn *Moby Dick* and *The Portrait of a Lady*. Gay culture is all around you—and it belongs to everybody.

BRUCE BAWER

It takes no compromise to give people their rights . . . it takes no money to respect the individual. It takes no political deal to give people freedom. It takes no survey to remove repression.

HARVEY MILK

CHAPTER FOUR

LOVE
and
FRIENDSHIP

"I just got another love letter from Barbara.
It's hard having a long distance relationship!"

The only queer people are the ones who don't love anybody.

When it comes, will it come without warning,
Just as I'm picking my nose?
Will it knock on my door in the morning,
Or tread in the bus on my toes?
Will it come like a change in the weather?
Will its greeting be courteous or rough?
Will it alter my life altogether?
O tell me the truth about love.

W. H. AUDEN

Everybody's journey is individual. You don't know with whom you're
going to fall in love. . . . If you fall in love with a boy, you fall in love with a boy.

JAMES BALDWIN

The lover is a friend inspired by God.

PLATO

Queer
Notions
page 76

Look, the way I figure it, today everything is so tough with trying to
find jobs and being as successful as your parents—to let love pass by because of
something like labels or someone's sex just seems really stupid.

DEBI BEATTY

Love is love. We're told little boys should love little girls and little girls should love little boys. We know it's not so.

JULIE HARRIS

In itself, homosexuality is as limiting as heterosexuality:
the ideal should be to be capable of loving a woman or a man; either,
a human being, without feeling fear, restraint or obligation.

SIMONE DE BEAUVOIR

The noble lover of beauty engages in love wherever he sees excellence and splendid
natural endowment without regard for any difference in physiological detail.

PLUTARCH

Our culture's ongoing refusal to acknowledge as moral and ordinary the
great variety of human love has distorted our understanding of reality and allowed
bigots to label as sick the most ordinary stirrings of the heart.

BLANCHE WIESEN COOK

It is so true that a woman may be in love with a woman, and a man with a man. It is pleasant to be sure of it, because it is undoubtedly the same love that we shall feel when we are angels.

MARGARET FULLER

Are there many things in this cool-hearted world so utterly exquisite as the pure love of one woman for another?

MARY MACLANE

The love expressed between women is particular and powerful, because we have had to love in order to live; love has been our survival.

AUDRE LORDE

There's something about the beauty and power of gay love. We build bridges between our differences, and honor the mystery of what we have.

MARK THOMPSON

The wonderful thing about queer relationships is that they are outside the jurisdiction of straight society.

ANONYMOUS

Gay people . . . enjoy greater fluidity in their relations as they explore a continuum ranging from lust to love to nurture to mentorship to friendship in the search for a new kind of family.

FRANK BROWNING

he tries to find his lips in the lips of other young men, he longs to feel his kind of love once more.

CONSTANTINE CAVAFY

Whenever the lover of boys . . . has the good fortune to encounter his own actual half, affection and kinship and love combined inspire in him an emotion which is quite overwhelming. . . .

ARISTOPHANES

. . . of two simple men I saw today on the pier in the midst of the crowd, parting the parting of dear friends, the one to remain hung on the other's neck and passionately kissed him.
While the one to depart tightly pressed the one to remain in his arms.

WALT WHITMAN

LOVE AND
FRIENDSHIP
page 79

There is never a day passes but what I think of you.

FRED VAUGHN, IN A LETTER TO WALT WHITMAN

Threads of manly friendship, fond and loving, pure and sweet, strong and life-long, carried to degrees hitherto unknown. . . .

HERMAN MELVILLE

If we could somewise contrive to have a city or an army composed of lovers and those they loved, they could not be better citizens of their country than by thus refraining from all that is base in a mutual rivalry for honor; and such men as these, when fighting side by side, one might almost consider able to make even a little band victorious over all the world.

PHAEDRUS

If ever I have an enemy, let him love girls; let him delight in a boy if ever I have a friend!

SEXTUS PROPERTIUS

You must know that I am, of all men who were ever born, the most inclined to love persons. Whenever I behold someone who possesses any talent or displays any dexterity of mind, who can do or say something more appropriately than the rest of the world, I am compelled to fall in love with him; and then I give myself up to him so entirely that I am no longer my own property, but wholly his.

MICHELANGELO

I'm a gay man who loves gay men. If I could spend every hour of every day surrounded only by gay men, I would. If that's limited, if that's being a separatist; then I guess I'm limited and I guess I'm a separatist.

LOWELL BEAN

As gay men, we're much luckier, we have real friends.

MARK FISHER

My family of friends has kept me alive through lovers who have left, enterprises that have failed, and all too many stories that never got finished. That family has been part of remaking the world for me.

DOROTHY ALLISON

. . . I laugh and fall dreaming again
of the desire to show you to everyone I love,
to move openly together
in the pull of gravity, which is not simple,
which carries the feathered
grass a long way down the upbreathing air.

ADRIENNE RICH

I miss you even more than I could have believed; and I was prepared to
miss you a good deal. So this letter is just really a squeal of pain. It is incredible
how essential to me you have become. . . . I shan't make you love me any more
by giving myself away like this—But oh my dear, I *can't* be clever and
stand-offish with you: I love you too much for that.

VITA SACKVILLE-WEST, IN A LETTER TO VIRGINIA WOOLF

If a straight woman falls
in love with me, she must really love me.
If a gay woman loves me,
she's just a lesbian looking for a girlfriend.

SARAH SCHULMAN

The last relationship I was in, the woman was reading *Journey of Solitude* and I was reading *Permanent Partners*, so it doesn't surprise me that things didn't work out.

KAREN WILLIAMS

Heavens above! The reason why I'm so jealous of you is obvious enough! If you weren't so damned attractive physically, do you think my heart would beat almost to suffocation whenever I see you speak to someone?

VIOLET TREFUSSIS, IN A LETTER TO VITA SACKVILLE-WEST

I don't like the strong, silent type.
I like 'em weak and chatty.

GARY GALBRAITH

What is straight-acting? Is effeminacy an act? Is it inborn? Isn't it up to the person to handle? Is there anything to handle?

DAN BUTLER

I think people who make checklists
are the most miserable and alone because they
are looking for the perfect Entenmann's
that is delicious and has no calories.
Please, you want a brunette with a sense of humor,
a doctorate and HIV-negative status?
Good luck, honey. Love isn't so frequent that
you can put conditions on it.

PAUL RUDNICK

There was something stubborn in me that didn't want to lose weight to
attract a man. If the right man came along, he'd be able to see my virtues magically.
Once he kissed me, the frog would turn into a prince. I had become a trick question,
a heavy disguise, but behind the disobliging exterior was the welcoming child
I would always be. Of course, what I'd forgotten was that he was not Parsifal and
I was not the Grail; the medievalism of my imagination was not sufficiently up-to-date
to recognize that the lover was a shopper and I a product.

EDMUND WHITE

**Perfect ideals don't exist.
What does exist are healthy, available people
who are workable marriage material.**

RONNY GALICKI

Isn't it strange that when we fall in love, this great dream we have,
this extraordinary disease, it's inevitably with some perfectly ordinary person
who for some reason we cannot define is the magic bearer, the magician,
the one who brings all this to us. Why?

ANDREW HOLLERAN

*I know love is blind, but does it have
to be stupid as well?*

MATTHEW GARCIA

I'm through with [seeking out] love. I'm tired of going out
and wondering if I'm wearing the right cologne, if my hair is
cut just right, worrying if I have holesin my underwear.

RAAN MEDLEY

A lover is hardest to find when it's your
whole reason for existence.

BAMBI SUE BRICKOWSKY

I found myself in a position where
someone was actually
after me. It was so new and different
I didn't know what to do.

JAMES TURCOTTE

Our relationship didn't begin till I was nearly fifty. It's not a transitory thing.
We both know it's for life, and I think we're very privileged.

NIGEL HAWTHORNE, ON HIS LIFE PARTNER

It took us awhile—about eighteen years—
to work out our problems. But now everything is fine.
Sometimes, you just have to give things time.

CHUCK ADAMS

LOVE AND
FRIENDSHIP
page 87

I am learning that when he doesn't come home he is having a good time and yes that is unfaithful, but the earth so desperately needs good times, unfaithfulness, and water.

CHARLES ORTLIEB

Complete possession is proved only by giving all. All that you are unable to give possesses you.

ANDRÉ GIDE

A relationship should be part of your life, not your life.

WILDE SIDE MAGAZINE

We'll fuck in the snow and come in for tea safe in the winter harbor of the heart . . . men can love like that.

PAUL MONETTE

Men are men and their reasons for staying or leaving are the same whether they're gay or straight.

SYDNEY BIDDLE BARROWS

There is this illusion that homosexuals only have sex and heterosexuals fall in love.

BOY GEORGE

Do you really think that because we're gay, young and urban
we don't have the same need for fidelity and intimacy that any other
human beings do? When sex is as easy to get as a burger at McDonald's,
it ain't too mysterious or marvelous, believe me.

ANDREW HOLLERAN

While dykes struggle to decide whether to celebrate the day they met,
their first date, their first sex act, or the date they fell in love,
gay men generally do not have this dilemma, because all of these
events took place on the same glorious day.

MERYL COHN

In the lesbian nursing home, my dearest one, There'll be soft
flannel sheets on the double bed. We'll lock our bedroom door.

CAROLYN CUTTER

The idea that the more deeply one loves, the more one opens oneself to
ultimate pain and suffering is one with which I agree completely.
Recognizing that fact and choosing to love anyway takes courage and maturity.

BOB SATULOFF

Afraid of losing you

I ran fluttering

like a little girl

after her mother

SAPPHO

*The inner voice tells us that our feelings
of love are righteous.
Black men loving black men is
indeed a sacred act.*

RON SIMMONS

I say if it's love the Lord won't mind.

GORDON MERRICK

What we are is a crime, if it is a crime to love, for the god who made me made me love.

PAUL-JACQUES-AIMÉ BAUDRY

I am the love that dare not speak its name.

LORD ALFRED BRUCE DOUGLAS

It is that deep spiritual affection that is as pure as it is perfect. It is beautiful, it is fine, it is the noblest form of affection. There is nothing unnatural about it.

OSCAR WILDE

I just want to be loved. Is that so wrong?

HARVEY FIERSTEIN

Love him . . . love him and let him love you.
Do you think anything else under heaven really matters?

JAMES BALDWIN

CHAPTER FIVE

SEX
and
BEAUTY

"Lookin' sharp, handsome!"

Homosexuality is not an affliction, and by God,
we're going to enjoy it.

FRANK KAMENY

*The only unnatural sex act is that
which you cannot perform.*

ALFRED KINSEY

Sins of the flesh are listed as crimes against nature, as abnormal,
and as perversions of nature's intent—as if there were some source other
than nature from which they could have come.

C. A. TRIPP

The experience of physical love between two people of either the same or the
opposite sex is to be engaged in and enjoyed for its own sake.

VATSYANA

Gays are in the vanguard of that final divorce of sex from conventional notions of sin.

ANNE RICE

I believe that sexual desire is a powerful emotion and a healthy one.
I'm pretty sure that when anyone acknowledges and acts on their desire,
it does us all some good—even if only by giving other people permission to act
on their desire—that it is sexual repression that warps desire and hurts people.

DOROTHY ALLISON

*In America sex is an obsession,
in the rest of the world it is a fact.*

MARLENE DIETRICH

A vast amount of nonsensical research continues to be conducted into
"the gay lifestyle" by people who presumably would scoff at the notion that all
heterosexuals share an identical way of life. In reality, gay men experience sex
in as many ways as everyone else, ways which change over time.

SIMON WATNEY

To judge from French novels, it's always a case of copulation or nothing;
to judge from English novels; it's always a case of nothing.
And then, the moralists—but they, poor dears, can hardly be expected
to throw much light on such a subject.

LYTTON STRACHEY

We acknowledge the gaily erotic nature of all things
and we reject the forcible attempts of straight society . . .
to define and thereby limit the human experience.

LES PETITES BONBONS

*I was once asked whether my
first sexual encounter was homosexual
or heterosexual. I don't know.
I was too polite to ask.*

GORE VIDAL

I love your innocence. Let's go play with it.

ROD HAYES

I went home with this guy and I didn't want to
but you know how it is; sometimes you just get hungry.

KEITH ROBINSON

Oh! If only we were naked now, and free
To watch our protruding parts align;
To whisper—both of us—in ecstacy!

Arthur Rimbaud

When a gay man goes out for anonymous sex,
he is often really seeking intimacy
and acceptance, even if he doesn't actually
receive either of those things.

WALT ODETS

When one wants to give normal young men lingering kisses
on the mouth and endless talk about eternal friendship one must know that a
soldier offering himself in a pub for a quick wank at ten shillings a time
is unlikely to be suitable.

HARRY DALEY

A number of these sailors were with other men
walking arm in arm, and on one dark street I saw
a sailor and a man kissing each other. . . .
Some of the sailors told me that they might be able
to get a girl if they went "up-town" but it was too far up
and they were too drunk to go way up there.

ANONYMOUS

This Y.M.C.A. is for transients but one further uptown
is a more elegant brothel, for those who like to live in their ivory towers with
Greek gods. If you go to the shower there is always someone
waiting to have an affair. It doesn't take long.

PAUL HOEBER

I felt very close to God. . . .
My friends say that's because I was always on my knees.

ARMISTEAD MAUPIN

Today's trick is tomorrow's competition.

ANONYMOUS

Of course, recycling is nothing new to New York City's gay men.
We've been reusing each other's tricks and lovers for years.
Paper and plastic, that's how we separate them;
the ones with the bills and the ones with the credit cards.

KENNY DASH

Recently I've begun to realize that the number of hot men I can get
into bed is much larger than the number of hot men whose company warrants
pretending I'm interested in their lives.

STEVE MOORE

My tragedy is that I cannot follow my instincts—too sophisticated
to obey them, not too sophisticated not to hear them.

ALAIN LOCKE

Sometimes the men I date are merely too young, which is another way of saying that they make me feel too old.

JAFFE COHEN

When I was younger I fancied older men, but now I find myself fancying younger men.
Right now, I think I can fancy anything that vaguely moves.

KEVIN ELYOT

I was susceptible to the prettiness of some fifteen-year-olds.

EVELYN WAUGH

I should compare him to a profusion of cherry or pear blossoms, in the haze of a spring
dawn, that is how he captivates, with the blossoming of his appearance.

NIJO YOSHIMOTO

There are so many goddamn models here in New York,
but sometimes I'll see a boy on the street
and I get that sense of wonder. It's really the difference
between going to a florist and finding a wildflower.

CHRISTOPHER MAKOS

Graceful son of Pan . . . your cloven hooves glisten. Your chest resembles
a cithara, and jingling bells ring in your blonde arms. Your heart beats
in your belly, where a double sex lies sleeping.

ARTHUR RIMBAUD

All that cannot be explained makes me holy—
my arrival, my nature, my skin, my gold hair, my eyes,
my placid acceptance of all attentions and offerings.

ROBERT FERRO

*You get beautiful by only
thinking of you.*

DAN BUTLER

Money makes you beautiful.

MADONNA

Lesbians find themselves right in the middle of the classic beauty argument. Some dykes find the *Playboy* woman to be their ideal, and others find her to be an ideal but they feel guilty about her.

SUSIE BRIGHT

I got so accustomed to being with women who wore scrubbed faces that I found I couldn't bring myself to kiss a woman in lipstick. It felt so wrong!

JEANNE CORDOVA

It may be different for gay women, but I think as a whole, gay men are very fucked up about looks. And I think they would agree with me, too.

SANDRA BERNHARD

What a handsome face he had: but if he were naked you would forget he had a face, he is so beautiful in every way.

PLATO

The figure is more important than the face,
and more important than the figure is the means by which you keep it.

COCO CHANEL

One should either be a work of art, or wear a work of art.

OSCAR WILDE

The most beautiful thing there is, is a naked man.

THOMAS EAKINS

We love men.
We just don't want to see them naked.

TWO NICE GIRLS

I take no pleasure in women . . . but men's bodies, in repose or in movement,
especially the former, appeal to me directly and very generally.

T. E. LAWRENCE

I have to admit that I don't know much about female anatomy.
I deal with most things on a need to know basis so, in fact, I may never know.

STEPHEN CARTER

Women alone stir my imagination.

VIRGINIA WOOLF

Between women love is contemplative; caresses are intended less to
gain possession of the other than gradually to re-create the self through her. . . .

SIMONE DE BEAUVOIR

Men who are obsessed with sex are convinced
that Lesbians are obsessed with sex.
Actually, like any other women, we are obsessed
with love and fidelity.

JUDY GRAHN

The lover takes courage in her certainty of caressing a body whose secrets
she knows, whose preferences her own body has taught her.

COLETTE

And here the smiling young girl who does
not want anything foreign in her body,
who wants neither him nor anything of him,
who wants only mine. . . .

MARINA TSVETAYEVA

She initiated me, as surely as any high priestess, into the wonders of
a woman's powers. She would lay her soft, curvy, naked woman's body on the bed,
place her hands behind her head, and unconsciously flex a brace of brawny biceps.

BARBARA SMITH

The surprise and delight of making love to her that night still fills me.
What was supposed to be queer, perverted and debased was, I found, lovely,
sacred, and healing. Even in our virgin awkwardness, I felt alive and
radiantly welcomed into another's arms, mind, and body.

NANCY L. WILSON

When I finally realized that I didn't want to be a butch,
I wanted to sleep with a butch,
a whole new world opened up before my eyes.

LESLEA NEWMAN

*I became a Lesbian because
of women, because women are beautiful,
strong and compassionate.*

RITA MAE BROWN

Heterosexuality is a serious health hazard for women at this point in time.

FRANCES HORNSTEIN

Particularly for a young woman in a world of AIDS,
I've said [lesbianism] seems to be a safer way to explore your
sexuality, rather than screwing around with a lot of boys.

CINDY CRAWFORD

A National Lesbian Purity Board is called for in this time of wavering allegiance to the cunt.
Laminated identity cards with small, colorful photographs could easily fit into one's wallet.
And random vaginal smears would be helpful in culling impostors from the ranks.

MARY WINGS

*Safe sex sucks, but is our only
alternative for now.*

ANONYMOUS

Unsafe sex is both suicidal and homicidal.

RONNY GALICKI

Heterosexual pundits often casually suggest that we
give up anal sex altogether,
as if this were like giving up sweets for Lent.

KIKI MASON

Where sex talk is concerned, we all know folks who blush and blanche at the
mention of words like dick and pussy in polite discourse, but who relish
putting their lips on the very genitalia those terms describe.

GREG TATE

To write about homosexual practices without dealing
with anal intercourse would be equivalent
to writing a history of music and omitting Mozart.

RONALD HAWKINS

O my friends can there be an extravagance to equal that of imagining that
a man must be a monster deserving to lose his life because he has preferred enjoyment
of the asshole to that of the cunt, because a young man with whom he finds
two pleasures, those of being at once lover and mistress, has appeared to him
preferable to a young girl, who promises but half as much?

MARQUIS DE SADE

SEX AND
BEAUTY
page 109

People say I'm a pain in the ass.
But there are good pains in the ass and bad pains in the ass.

STAN LEVENTHAL

It hurt but it was a good hurt.

LOUIS RODRIGUEZ

If a man has intercourse with the hindquarters of his equal [male], that man will be foremost among [his] brothers and colleagues.

THE SUMMA ALU

I'm always amazed at the American practice of allowing one party to a
homosexual act to remain passive—it's so undemocratic.

W. H. AUDEN

Tops need to be more aggressive about asking for what we want and stop acting like
a bunch of victimized codependents held hostage by rapacious bottoms.

PAT CALIFIA

Nobody who's a bottom will ever say they are.

TED OTTAVIANO

Queer Notions
page 110

Remember, don't put candles, bottles,
light bulbs, or any other objects up your ass—
and don't let anyone else do it to you.

CHARLES SILVERSTEIN AND FELICE PICANO

You've got the leather harness, the cock ring, and the pierced nipple
(with optional chain connecting it artfully to your pierced nose).
You've shaved your back, polished your motorcycle boots and completed your
final tanning session. You might imagine that you're finally prepared for The Black
Party—but you're forgetting one final act of body mutilation. Like studded
armbands or vinyl jock straps, tattoos are all but a required accessory
for TBP, an act of permanent marking that separates the men from the boys.

PERRY MCMAHON

*The point is to live
in style, not drop dead in it.*

JAMES MERRILL

CHAPTER SIX

STRAIGHT FOLK

Mom, Dad, two kids: the American dream!

As a word for heterosexual . . . ["breeder"] implies that, while lesbians and gay men provide the world with wit and creativity, the production of children is the only really useful role of heterosexuality.

WILLIAM STEWART

Heterosexuals are the ungrateful children of gay culture.

HARVEY FIERSTEIN

If you removed homosexuals and homosexual influence from what is generally regarded as American culture, you would be pretty much left with *Let's Make a Deal*.

FRAN LEBOWITZ

Heterosexuality is a boring and horrible lifestyle.

EDITH MASSEY

Gay people are not in the habit of thinking of ourselves as leading our civilization, and yet we do.

JUDY GRAHN

Queer
Notions

The immensity of the debt that Western civilization owes to gay and lesbian genius is pretty ironic, given that homosexuality is often described as a threat to Western civilization.

BRUCE BAWER

Any magazine of the cutting edge of taste or fashion is going to recruit—either consciously or unconsciously—a gay sensibility. We were born to create trends, that's what we do well.

KEVIN SESSUMS

[Gay people] pick up on things faster than straight mainstream America does.

FRANK DECARO

Most gay bashers will be wearing what gay people had on four years earlier—only in polyester with a Penney's label.

PAUL RUDNICK

The secret weapon of heterosexuality is children. Their needs consume all resources, conversational topics and attention spans. We couldn't talk about gender issues. We couldn't even play a game of twenty questions with any assurance. It's hard to talk political agenda when your primary focus is a two-year-old choking on a Ninja in the way-back seat.

JOHN WEIR

The way straight people see it, they're raising the next generation of factory workers so they don't have much sympathy for frivolous, shopping homosexuals and greedy lesbians with two houses.

JAMES TURCOTTE

I like straight people.
I just don't want them teaching our kids.

SUZANNE WESTENHOEFER

Straight America is waking up to the fact that its culture is not monolithic.

ROBIN STEVENS

If you're straight then I'm crooked, but if I'm gay then you're morose.

ROBIN TYLER

I'm not a straight man, but I play one on television.

DAN BUTLER

All men are homosexual, some of them turn straight. It must be very odd to be a straight man, because your sexuality is hopelessly defensive.

DEREK JARMAN

We're so inured to the sight of straight men responding violently to the mere idea of another man finding them attractive that we don't pause to consider how bizarre this reaction is.

MICHAEL LEWIS

It may be an academically interesting puzzle as to why we are gay . . . but it is much more interesting and important to find out why people are homophobic.

PETER NARDI

STRAIGHT
FOLK
page 117

The dread of homosexuality is a result of, and derives its tremendous force from, the wishes for the homosexual expression which are present in our unconscious minds.

MARTIN HOFFMAN

[The] main reason for the tremendous popularity of football in America may be our subconscious fascination over the fact that each play starts with the quarterback squatting between the center's legs in the classic pose of sodomy.

NORMAN MAILER

Identifying straight men as the profiteers behind homophobia, rather than realizing that they are its fellow victims, has diverted the gay movement from recognizing an important ally.

FREDRIC HAYWARD

Some men may find the business of deflecting unwanted homosexual attention disturbing not because they are secretly gay but because they consider all "female" roles degrading.

MICHAEL LEWIS

Queer Notions
page 118

If boys are better, why should a male choose
to love an "inferior" female? If a penis is so great,
two penises should be even greater.

LETTY COTTIN POGREBIN

What is most beautiful in virile men is
something feminine; what is most beautiful in feminine women
is something masculine.

SUSAN SONTAG

Princes cannot forget their pages even after they marry princesses. . . .
A sincere relationship between two males is true love.

IHARA SAIKAKU

*Like the great majority of men I've had
several homosexual experiences and I'm
not remotely ashamed of it.*

MARLON BRANDO

Bob and I were talking about how hard it was to find Ten Straight Men, and somebody said that that should be my next portfolio—ten men who've never had a homosexual experience.

ANDY WARHOL

Straight men need to be emasculated. . . . Every straight guy should have a man's tongue in his mouth at least once.

MADONNA

The only way to cure a homosexual of his foible is to make him love women . . . heterosexual men can be cured exactly in the same way from their love for women.

HENRY GERBER

Men think a woman homosexual could be turned around with by a good night in bed with a man.

GLORIA STEINEM

Look at lesbian chic. What's that all about? It's a straight-boy fantasy of what lesbianism really is.

LEA DELARIA

Girls who put out are tramps. Girls who don't are ladies. This is, however, a rather archaic usage of the word. Should one of you boys happen upon a girl who doesn't put out, do not jump to the conclusion that you have found a lady. What you have probably found is a Lesbian.

FRAN LEBOWITZ

After a lifetime of dealing with straight men, straight women find lesbian advances a cinch.

MICHAEL LEWIS

Johnny, you're my favorite straight man and I've known my share of straight men.

BETTE MIDLER, TO JOHNNY CARSON

I saw this psychiatrist on Barbara Walters who said he could make gay men straight. He said he was going to make every gay man straight. Barbara looked horrified. "Who's going to do my hair, who's going to decorate my living room? Save two big old queens for me, I'll pay."

FRANK MAYA

CHAPTER SEVEN

FAMILY MATTERS

"Could I borrow the car tonight, Dad? I have a date with Roger!"
"Sure, son! And here's ten bucks."

Home is where the heart is, no matter how the heart lives.

SALLY FINGERETT

Family life has nothing to do with sexual preference.

RALPH BLUMENTHAL

For death, or life, or toil,
To thee myself I join;
I take thy hand in mine,
With thee I would grow old.

FROM AN ANCIENT CHINESE MALE-MALE
UNION CEREMONY

He pressed his forehead against mine, clasped me around my waist, and said henceforth we were married.

HERMAN MELVILLE

New laws of love to link and intertwine
Majestic peoples; Love to weld and weave
Comrade to comrade, man to bearded man, . . .

WALT WHITMAN

Marriage is the only acceptable route to stemware.
PAUL RUDNICK

Marriage is a long, dull meal with dessert served at the beginning.
OSCAR WILDE

We recognize that families have changed, and our benefits are becoming more flexible as we move toward more choice for all Xerox people, whatever their family circumstances.
BRENT LAYMON

Our society's foundation, its very bedrock has been shaken by the realization of gay and lesbian parenthood.
LAURA BENKOW

There are an estimated eight to ten million children being raised in three million gay- and lesbian-headed households in the United States.
TEACHERS COLLEGE RECORD

Why are we campaigning to join the military and adopt children?
I thought one of the few advantages of being gay was
not being expected to do that kind of shit.

BOB PEALOLA

This whole family concept is so completely out-of-date. Sociologically, biologically,
every other way, that is not the way things are gonna go. This stupid, failing family nonsense,
baby—that just isn't the way things are going. Things don't go backwards.

WILLIAM BURROUGHS

Your family are the people who love you.

MARK LUKENS

*Gay, Lesbian, Bi, and Straight,
we are the community and family of God,
and we are here knowing God loves us.*

NATHAN BAXTER

When I think of the family and friends whose respect I have earned by being honest,
then I am grateful to be gay because I'm grateful to be myself and to be loved for it.

ARNIE KANTROWITZ

It wasn't easy telling my family that I'm gay. I made my carefully worded announcement at Thanksgiving. It was very Norman Rockwell. I said, "Mom would you please pass the gravy to a homosexual?" She passed it to my father. A terrible scene followed.

Bob Smith

For the homos who go home for the holidays,
there are always tales to tell. For the
last two years, I've been trying a non-interventionist
strategy. Basically, it consists of keeping
conversation centered on compelling discussion
of the food and the weather.

LAURA COTTINGHAM

I'll never forget watching TV with my parents the night of the fire at the Continental Baths
and seeing my boyfriend, having just escaped through a window dressed only in a
towel and flip-flops, being interviewed by a local news reporter. "Why is that boy only
wearing a towel?" my mother asked. "Uhhh . . . ," was my quick-witted response.

BRUCE EDWARD HALL

We all have pictures of our daughters. In my mind,
Michelle was in the city or country, and she had a dog and
a husband and children. To throw another woman in there,
I just didn't think about it that way.

AN OLEY

"You are not a lesbian!"
"Yes mother, I am!"
"You don't actually sleep with
other girls, do you?"
"How else could I be a lesbian?"

ANDY WARHOL

My mother said to me, "Why do you have to call yourself
a dyke? Why can't you be a nice lesbian?"
"Because I'm not a nice lesbian, I'm a big dyke."

LEA DELARIA

No, mother I'm not gay but I have decided to adopt the gay lifestyle.

ROBERT PADILLA

All I know is this: If you and Papa are responsible for the way I am,
then I thank you with all of my heart, for it is the light and the joy of my life.

ARMISTEAD MAUPIN

*The gay gene is a myth created by
mothers of homosexuals.*

PAUL WALKER

In [my parents'] generation homosexuality didn't exist and if it did exist,
we were monsters. That's the way it is. They don't even have words to discuss it.
With their friends they don't even know how to discuss me being gay
because they don't have the words. All the words they do have are things like
"pervert," "monster," "creep," and "queer."

SCOTT THOMPSON

Growing up a lesbian in a family full of Pentecostal ministers was like being an Eskimo who landed in the middle of the Sahara desert.

AYOFEMI FOLAYAN

My father is a retired Air Force Colonel. When I was growing up, known homosexuals were literally not allowed in the house.

ANDREW C. M. COILE

One of the most painful aspects of life for hundreds and thousands of gays and lesbians has been the forced exile brought on by being rejected from our families, and those institutions and supports that are our birthrights. . . .

VIRGINIA APUZZO

When a young black man goes to jail because he's stolen a car, or he's become a drug dealer in our community, there is one place he can always go. He can always go home again. No matter if he's become a thief, if he's strayed from the path, his mama will take him home again. Let me tell you what happens if he comes out as gay: He can't go home again.

PHILL WILSON

FAMILY MATTERS
page 131

I never actually came out to them in that TV-movie way; it's more an unspoken thing. I went out with a guy for three years and they met him— and mothers always know.

GREGG ARAKI

Looking back I wonder if I didn't do it a tiny bit to spite my mother.

CHRISTOPHER ISHERWOOD

Gay men and straight men have much more in common than do gay men
with lesbians or straight men with straight women.
Every man must define his identity against his mother. If he does not,
he just falls back into her and is swallowed up.

CAMILLE PAGLIA

The other day there was a guy driving me from Nashua College whose brother
is gay and has AIDS, and won't tell his parents. And I said,
"Look, tell your brother to tell your mom. Mothers will love you regardless."

ARTHUR ASHE

The AIDS crisis, I had thought, was happening all around me—
but to other people, not to my family.

ANN HERMAN

Months after Bobby's death, my mother wept as she prepared breakfast. When my father
asked, "Are you alright?" she said, "Yes, of course. I always cry when I poach eggs."

BARBARA LAZEAR ASCHER

That is everybody's nightmare—to die and your mother has the last word.

SARAH SCHULMAN

CHAPTER EIGHT

HONEY,

a Dollar is a Dollar

"I spent so much on clothes, facials, manicures, and
hair-care products this month, there's hardly any left for food.
Oh well, I'm on a diet anyway!"

The gay and lesbian liberation movement has turned into the gay and lesbian marketing movement.

MARC STEIN

Our leaders are no longer intellectuals but marketers.

SARAH SCHULMAN

In America, sex, money and power are paramount. Not that that's so different from anyplace else but I do think we're a bit more hypocritical about it.

STUART MACK

People are pooh-poohing events where you only raise $5,000 or $10,000, saying it's as easy to throw an event where people pay $50 as $5. Not everyone can pay $150 for a ticket.

MARC BERKLEY

Queer
Notions
page 136

**HONEY,
A DOLLAR
IS A DOLLAR**
page 137

No one just gives parties anymore. I mean, what do people do besides go to benefits? It seems you're either with the three people who are the most important to you in the whole world or you're at a benefit.

MARISA CARDINALE

It is easy to be independent when you've got money. But to be independent when you haven't got a thing—that's the Lord's test.

MAHALIA JACKSON

You've got to have something to eat and a little love in your life before you can hold still for any damn body's sermon on how to behave.

BILLIE HOLIDAY

What am I supposed to say "I'm a lesbian, leave me alone?"
How far am I gonna get with that?

A NEW YORK CITY WAITRESS, ON WHY SHE FLIRTS WITH MALE CUSTOMERS

She turned down my book because she thought it was too gay.
She said that when you're an editor at a major publishing house you have to be
careful in guarding your position. I'm glad she's guarding her position so well.

FELICE PICANO, ON HEARING THAT THE EDITOR IN QUESTION WAS FIRED

I don't want no shade. I just want to get paid.

RUPAUL

I love my character Mamaw, and if she helps to pay the bills, that's fine. If somebody's
willing to pay a cover charge to see her, I'm willing to bring her out. Anything that gets
me out of waiting tables. I'm too old to be a prostitute. And so is Mamaw.

GARY GALBRAITH

There are tons of drag queens out there who will perform for beer nuts and
a subway token. And where does that leave me, huh? Poor, penniless and insane!
I'm not paranoid, I'm just preparing for my inevitable future.

HEDDA LETTUCE

In Hollywood, the route to freedom is always financial.

PAUL RUDNICK

Always put sex and violence in your films.
That way, even if it's no good
at least somebody will want to see it.

JOHN WATERS

Having sex and representing it on film is not a turn-on. It's work.

BRUCE LABRUCE

Working as a male prostitute is a job here, not necessarily a sexual orientation.

A THAI PROSTITUTE

*I do want to get rich but I never want
to do what there is to do to get rich.*

GERTRUDE STEIN

Honey, a dollar is a dollar. Don't worry about where it came from.
The landlord don't care where you get it as long as you got it.

ED DAVIS

**HONEY,
A DOLLAR
IS A DOLLAR**
page 139

CHAPTER NINE

CITY LIVING

Night clubs, restaurants, galleries, theater—the city has it all!

I have never felt salvation in nature.
I love cities above all.

MICHELANGELO

The city is the human market-place that allows strange people to seek out those of fellow-feeling, it offers economic independence, the anonymity and randomness needed to sponsor original styles of life.

EDMUND WILSON

New York used to be a magnet. Why did we move here? I can imagine, with very few exceptions, that everyone moved to New York from a prettier place. We didn't move here for quality of life. We moved here for life.

FRAN LEBOWITZ

While I lived in New York, I did not have any long-term relationships. Perhaps I was not ready. Perhaps it had something to do with the very nature of a city filled with innumerable choices, where people fly like moths at night from flame to flame in search of the ever more satisfying.

MIKE GILBERTO

Queer
Notions
page 142

How many straight New York City waiters
does it take to change a light bulb? Both of them.

ANONYMOUS

Everyone in New York is gay. Didn't you know?
Most of the rest of the world is too but,
except for San Francisco, they're too scared to admit it.

STEPHANIE STRONG

The gay communities in both Australia and in Britain really look to what we are doing,
particularly here in New York, to set the standards. We set the political and activist
standards. You start to realize what incredible importance what we do here in New York
has when you see people wearing David Spada's Freedom rings in Glasgow.

DAVID DRAKE

Like every other sub-population in American history,
gay people of the last quarter century have staked out their
geographical turf—specific districts in New York
and San Francisco, Houston and Chicago and Los Angeles.

FRANK BROWNING

It happens all the time. . . . Gay people come to a neighborhood and make it fabulous. Then heterosexual people come in and trailer-trash it and we move on.

MARK NELSON

Brooklyn isn't the easiest place to grow up, especially if you're a homo.

MICHELANGELO SIGNORILE

There ain't nothing for us in Brooklyn. They're just gonna put us on a raft and send us to Jersey. Dance while you float.

MARK BROWN

Back in Philly, it was rough. If you were a queen and you wanted to carry a purse, you'd better have a .38 in it.

JOHN BOWMAN

Men from L.A. ask for what they want. And, with me, they get it.

JAMES TURCOTTE

CITY
LIVING
page 145

In L.A., there's definitely a stigma attached
to being a drag queen.
Forget doing drag and having a boyfriend.

SHERRY VINE

The road of a gay man through Washington politics is rocky and tough.
One of the first things he develops antennae for is whether there is hostility
toward him solely on the basis of his sexual orientation.

W. SCOTT THOMPSON

The best homosexuality is in America, like the best everything else,
and California, where all national tendencies achieve their
most hyperbolic expression, is a living beach of writhing male bodies.

ANTHONY BURGESS

. . . it's like San Francisco; you can walk around all day and never have to talk
to a straight person. Sometimes you wonder "What are straight people thinking
and doing?"; but that's usually a passing thought.

JACK THOMAS

I just got back from San Francisco. It's like a gay Disneyland.

FRANK MAYA

San Francisco is a refugee camp for homosexuals. We have fled here
from every part of the nation, and like refugees elsewhere, we came not because
it was so great here, but because it was so bad there.

CARL WITTMAN

As much as we have issues with Middle America stereotyping gays, it's equally true that gays stereotype what goes on in Middle America.

BRUCE COHEN

The days are gone when everything is happening in New York or San Francisco.

DIDIER HEIREMANA

You know, the city doesn't surrender all of her secrets at the first glance.

ROD HAYES

CHAPTER TEN

LIFE
in
WARTIME

"We finally made it, honey!"

Gay people are a people at war inside
a society at peace.

SCOTT THOMPSON

Outing is queer self-defense.

PETER TATCHELL

I'm a gay person so I don't live in a free country.

ANONYMOUS

Wherever it has been established that it is shameful to be involved in sexual
relationships with men, that is due to evil on the
part of the rulers, and to cowardice on the part of the governed.

PLATO

One cannot serve this Eros without becoming a
stranger in society as it is today; one cannot commit oneself
to this form of love without incurring a mortal wound.

THOMAS MANN

The enemy is everyone, gay or straight, who passively supports oppression by their silence.

Romanovsky and Phillips

On November 13th, 1895, I was brought down here from London.
From two o'clock till half-past two on that day I had to stand on the centre platform
of Clapham Junction in convict dress and handcuffed, for the world to look at. . . .
When people saw me they laughed. Each train as it came up swelled
the audience. Nothing could exceed their amusement. That was of course before
they knew who I was. As soon as they had been informed, they laughed still more.
For half an hour I stood there in the grey November rain surrounded
by a jeering mob. For a year after that was done to me I wept every day at
the same hour and for the same space of time.

OSCAR WILDE

Laws that are sex laws are not only aimed at homosexuals—sodomy laws, for example, are not advocated against just homosexuals—they are also advocated against heterosexuals. Basically, what we have now is a puritanical fascism in regard to all.

FRAN LEBOWITZ

The sporadic entrapment of gay men in public restrooms or parks is a good deal less
repressive than the systematic hunting down and discharging of homosexuals that we
require of our armed forces. But the differences are matters of degree rather than of kind.

ANDREW SULLIVAN

They're trying to take away my pride
They're trying to hurt me inside
I ain't been knocked down yet
I was born to fight

TRACY CHAPMAN

Heterosexuality has been forcibly and subliminally imposed on women.
Yet everywhere women have resisted it, often at the cost of physical torture,
imprisonment, psychosurgery, social ostracism, and extreme poverty.

ADRIENNE RICH

In Tinseltown, the rules were not the same for lesbians and gay men.
As long as a woman could show she was married or
occasionally available to men, lesbian affairs were more acceptable
in some circles than avant-garde art.

AXEL MADSEN

Among the dire results of my "unnaturalness" I had been told that I should go blind
and go mad. I believed this. In a kind of cold reasonableness, I triedto teach myself to
type and play the piano with my eyes shut, against the time I should go blind.

VALENTINE ACKLAND

**LIFE IN
WARTIME**
page 153

Cultural prejudice has not only succeeded in making most heterosexuals hate gays; it has succeeded in making most gay people hate themselves.

RANDY SHILTS

We, young and Black and fine and gay, sweated our first heartbreaks with no school or office chums to share that confidence over lunch hour. Just as there were no rings to make tangible the reason for our happy secret smiles, there were no names nor reason given or shared for the tears that messed up the lab reports or the library bills.

AUDRE LORDE

When people don't see themselves in the mass media, they often think, "Maybe this isn't real, maybe I am the only person going through this," only it is real and they're not the only one.

PATRICIA O'NEIL

It's tragic that there are some
who believe it isn't wrong to beat up
lesbians and gays. If any other
group was being deliberately killed,
there would be public outrage.

Dianne Hardy-Garcia

Gays and lesbians are the politically correct group to hate. If I went out
on a street corner and started shouting about hating Jews or blacks,
I would get in trouble. But I could go out to that same street corner and shout
anti-gay slogans and tap into thirty or forty percent of the population.

FLOYD COCHRAN

I won't be surprised the day a gay man takes out a gun
and shoots someone who's threatening his life. . . .
I think it's a viable self-defense option for many gay people.

ROBERT HILFERTY

When [former Reagan] Secretary [of Health and Human Services Margaret M.]
Heckler declared at an AIDS conference that we must stop the disease before it
spreads to the heterosexual population, she was only inadvertenly articulating the
general view that homosexuals live and die apart from the rest of us.

LARRY KRAMER

During the early days of the epidemic,
humor, sexuality, and even music seemed
questionable, in the face of so much horror.
They very quickly became essential.

PAUL RUDNICK

I'm laughing to keep from dying.

LANGSTON HUGHES

I had a self myself once but he died. When do we leave the mirror and lie down in front of the tanks? Let them put two million of us away; see how quickly it looks like Belsen.

PAUL MONETTE

I suppose it's not surprising that those who draw the connection between Jews and homosexuals are themselves Jewish homosexuals. It isn't surprising, but it is sad.

DAVID BERGMAN

Anyone who thinks of homosexual love is our enemy.

GERMAN NAZI PARTY

We use the pink and black triangles to remind us that all our lives and all our stories must never be forgotten if the atrocities of the past are to be never again.

KAREN PEPER

Apple pie, motherhood, and the American flag will not fall. We're already in the military.

MIRIAM BEN-SHALOM

The bitterest tears said over graves are for words left unsaid and deeds left undone.

HARRIET BEECHER STOWE

We often lose sight of the fact that a lot of homophobia just comes from sheer stupidity.

TOD ROULETTE

How can I feel hostility toward someone who's been misled by society to believe that hate and violence are synonymous with heroism?

AARON FRICKE

And now I will tell you what we want, we radical homosexuals: not for you to tolerate us, but to understand us. And this you can only do by becoming one with us.

MARTHA SHELLEY

We don't: carry weapons; "enforce laws;" or "clean up streets." We do:
intervenein bashings; stop anti-gay violence; cruise, dish, and window-shop shamelessly.

STREET PATROL, SAN FRANCISCO

Don't mess with the Gay Mafia—they'll break the legs on your coffee table. You could end up in the river wearing cement pumps.

BOB SMITH

Sometimes, younger guys ask me "Why does it have to be this way?"
All I can say is "I don't know, I don't know."

JAMES TURCOTTE

You deal with it. You don't ignore it; but you don't let it rule your life.

DAN BUTLER, ON DISCRIMINATION

The only way we can win this battle is to out-love those who oppose us.

MEL WHITE

We hugged each other in bed like brothers, but we were
too excited to sleep. We rushed down to buy the morning papers
to see how the Stonewall Uprising had been described.
"It's really our Bastille Day," Lou said. But we couldn't find a
single mention in the press of the turning point of our lives.

EDMUND WHITE

And so, the fight goes on.

BARNEY FRANK

CHAPTER ELEVEN

AIDS

"Where there's a will, there's a way.
If we all keep working together, we'll find a cure."

Grief should not be where
we have to start when we talk of sex.

DOROTHY ALLISON

We need to face the fact that when two gay men are in a room alone,
no matter what their status, there is a third person in the room. AIDS is kind of like
adultery, an unspoken thing that neither party forgets, even if it's not discussed.

ANONYMOUS

AIDS circumscribes the imagination;
there's no way around it. To write about sex
without mentioning AIDS is merely that:
to write about sex without mentioning AIDS.
AIDS is still there; it is merely unsaid.

DALE PECK

Well, everybody is worried about everybody now, that seems to
be the way we live, the way we live now.

SUSAN SONTAG

Queer
Notions
page 164

Not a day goes by that I don't think of the virus and cry for those who aren't so lucky.

MARK HALLO

It's hard to imagine life without the epidemic.

MICHAEL CUNNINGHAM

Whenever someone comes to me and says someone is sick
I think, "Who isn't?"

RAAN MEDLEY

Ten years ago if some 32-year-old fellow died, his whole friendship circle would
be devastated for years. They'd never get over it. Now it's so normal to die at 32.

SARAH SCHULMAN

Only clichés about "a new lease on life" and having
"a weight lifted off your shoulders" can describe being a 27-year-old
gay man in New York and testing negative.

MICHELANGELO SIGNORILE

One of the truths of testing HIV+ is that once you know, you can never not know again.

MICHAEL SLOCUM

Dating [as an HIV+ person] involves a complex set of maneuvers, because the stakes are so much higher. How do you come out for the second time, especially if you really like him? Do you divulge in between the appetizer and the main course, or do you wait until dessert?

KIKI MASON

I've never had a negative emotional exchange over my serostatus. I think part of that is my willingness to talk about it.

PHILL WILSON

AIDS is so pervasive; if anyone has a problem knowing about me, it's clearly theirs, not mine.

ROBERT WOOLLEY

Just remember those millions of people living successfully with HIV are people who've reached out to get the help they needed. Wherever you are, you can find support, or the means to create it. It just doesn't make sense for us to face the same issues without helping each other out. We are not alone. And neither are you.

JIM LEWIS

I don't feel any particular shame about having AIDS anymore.
I'm pissed off, and I'm sorry about it, but I don't feel any shame about it at all.
The time when one could die quietly in bed surrounded by
one's loved ones at the ripe age of eighty is gone. It's even gone for Reagan
now that he has Alzheimer's—though I don't know how they
can tell with him that he has Alzheimer's.

PAUL MONETTE

If he had measles,
it wouldn't matter where he got it.

PETER DAVIS

For the friend who still cannot be named—
and for all of us who live in a world where secrets must be kept.

AN INSCRIPTION ON THE AIDS QUILT

**What lengths, what depths they will go in their aversion!
The obituaries that refuse to list AIDS as the
cause of death—as if there were only one thing worse than
being dead and that is being homosexual.**

ANDREW HOLLERAN

AIDS
page 167

They tell me, "Let's do a story on fertility problems. A lot of our viewers at eleven have that problem." I say, "Shouldn't we be focusing on the most important health problems facing New Yorkers?" But I guess that would be redundant. If we did that all we'd ever be talking about would be AIDS.

STEPHEN GENDEL

M.D.s talk about AIDS constantly. Not tales of lovers legally and forcibly kept from the bedside, of the specifically horrible pain of an AIDS death, of the permanent sadness of losing a loved one, of the tragedy of no cure—no. They talk about how the pervasiveness of the AIDS devastation could be the catalyst to socialized medicine. And you know what that means: no more horse farms, tennis clubs, champagne and caviar.

LAURA COTTINGHAM

Corporate greed, government inaction, and public indifference make AIDS a political crisis.

GRAN FURY

Queer Notions

Yes, anger in and of itself can be seen as just one of the other great forces
or emotions. However, it's got to be harnessed. It's got to be understood. It's got to
be used and not be used by it. That's what I call wisdom.

BILL T. JONES

I came here today to ask that this nation with all its resources and compassion
not let my epitaph read he died of red tape.

ROGER LYON, ON HIS AIDS QUILT PANEL

*Wouldn't it be great if you could
only get AIDS by giving money
to television preachers?*

ELAYNE BOOSLER

I used to think that AIDS would change the world—
that we would finally shed all of our "isms"
and fight for our lives with mutual respect together.
Then again, I used to think Liberace was straight.

MICHAEL SLOCUM

As the AIDS crisis has so movingly shown, gay people have built the kind of community that evaporated for many non-gay Americans decades ago. You don't see straight volunteers queuing up to change cancer patients' bedpans and deliver their groceries.

JONATHAN RAUCH

They've been going through this for years and they've been really taking care of their own. You have to give the gay and lesbian community a lot of credit for that. The rest of us have a lot to learn from that.

MAGIC JOHNSON

It's not the disease, pussycat, it's what you do with it.

KIKI MASON

If AIDS has taught us anything, it is that we are the most tenacious, inspired, creative, committed survivors on the face of this earth.

ROGER MCFARLANE

Since I've had this I appreciate special days more—Thanksgiving, Christmas, my birthday. I celebrate every holiday as if it might be my last. And I know, pretty soon, one of them is going to be.

RICHARD IRIZARRY

I can usually tell someone's status before we discuss it. People with AIDS have a sense of urgency, a no-bullshit, get-on-with-my-life kind of attitude. There's an almost frantic energy about them. They're not engaged in long-term planning. It's a different way of thinking.

ANONYMOUS

After my father died, I had kept his morphine and pills. I had kept it because I thought I might need it to end my life in the event I got really sick. I got so depressed that I decided to use the morphine to see if it helped. The morphine did exactly what I needed it to do: it numbed the pain and left me feeling mildly euphoric. It's very embarrasing to admit I did this. It makes me feel very weak. It's also illegal.

GREG LOUGANIS

I want to be next to my loved ones after I die. The quilt is our family plot, you see. Many of us design our own panels before we die, but I think mine is the only blank space on the quilt. It's waiting for me.

Roxy Ventola

Live your life, focus on the living. The dying will take care of itself.

PHILL WILSON

I'm definitely dying; I know it in my bones, I can't say when, but soon.
And it's truly OK. I don't know how to break it to you, but we're all gonna eventually die.
Maybe not from AIDS, but there are a lot of buses out there to run people down.

MICHAEL CALLEN

There is a delightful freedom you feel when you realize it doesn't matter
if you die. It creates a bliss I enjoy every day of my life. If I get out of whack with
all this, I just remember, "Oh yeah, this is only a cosmic joke."

JOHN DUGDALE

During the run of "Jeffrey," some of our best audiences were made up of
elderly people, who were all too familiar with illness and the loss of friends. They were
blissfully irreverent; they knew that hospital gowns demand accessories.

PAUL RUDNICK

I am a contented person. I feel I've lived as long as I ought to live.
I've written my will. I'm not gloomy about death. The end of life makes old age more
acceptable and also, as it's toward the end of the run, you can overact appallingly.

QUENTIN CRISP

*I am sick and I may not be here
for the next one but if not
I'll be somewhere, somewhere listening
for my name.*

MELVIN DIXON

He was my North, my South, my East and West,
My morning week and my Sunday rest,
My noon, my midnight, my talk, my song; I thought
that love would last forever: I was wrong.

W. H. AUDEN

Bye sugar. Sorry it wasn't always sweet.

BRAD LAMM

AIDS
page 175

CHAPTER TWELVE

QUEERS *in* HISTORY

"The Queers are coming! The Queers are coming!"

We need rituals of memory among us.
We need ways of listening to each other about what
has really happened to us in the past. . . .

MINNIE BRUCE PRATT

That homosexuality has been a natural condition of kings, composers,
engineers, poets, housewives and bus drivers, and that it has contributed more than
its share of beauty and laughter to an ugly and ungrateful world should be
obvious to anyone who is willing to peer beneath the surface.

MARTIN GREIF

*The homosexual has been a significant
part of human sexuality since
the dawn of history, primarily because
it is an expression of capacities that
are basic in the human animal.*

ALFRED KINSEY

Queer
Notions
page 178

Many highly respectable individuals of ancient and modern times have been homosexual, several of the greatest among them (Plato, Michelangelo, Leonardo DaVinci, etc.).

SIGMUND FREUD

The fact that homosexuality is especially common among men of exceptional talent was long since noted by Dante. . . . There cannot be the slightest doubt that intellectual and artistic abilities of the highest order have frequently been associated with a congenially inverted sexual temperament.

HAVELOCK ELLIS

Respected and admired women, public women with power and prestige have been discussed for decades in terms of spinsterhood or loneliness, or in terms of "Boston marriages," by which we are meant to assume chaste, untouching companionship. The truth is merely that they were not public about their private lives. They lived in a world of coded words and costumes, a world of lavender and violets, pinkie rings and pearls.

BLANCHE WIESEN COOK

> *Might I remind you that the greatest artists and philosophers did not enjoy the benefits of heterosexuality?*
>
> PHILIP LARKIN

> When the lover is able to contribute towards wisdom and excellence,
> and the beloved is anxious to improve his education and knowledge in general,
> then and only then . . . is it honorable for a boy to yield to his lover.
>
> PLATO

> **Platonic love, in spite of the meaning commonly attributed to it,**
> **is a common search for truth and beauty by**
> **two persons of the same sex, inspired by mutual affection.**
>
> WALTER HAMILTON

> It is certain, as certain as knowledge of antiquity can be, that Socratic love
> was not a sordid love: this word love has deluded us. Those who were called the lover
> of young men were precisely those who are the minions of our princes today.
>
> VOLTAIRE

Richard [I] is said to have been homosexual, but if so, he didn't flaunt his preference. It may well be that in spite of his dazzlingly virile appearance, he just wasn't interested in sex—either of them. After all, sexual adventure, to a warrior, probably can't begin to compare with charging around slaughtering Muslims.

JANICE YOUNG BROOKS

Dapple-throned Aphrodite,
eternal daughter of God,
snare-knitter! Don't I beg you,
cow my heart with grief! Come. . . .

SAPPHO

But the [anti-sodomy] laws, ordinances and decrees were neither respected nor enforced, and that was because the persons responsible for their execution were themselves involved. . . .

GIROLAMO PRIULI

Buggery is now almost grown as common among our gallants as in Italy, and the very pages in this town begin to complain of their masters for it.

SAMUEL PEPYS

QUEERS
IN HISTORY
page 181

Speaking of bardashes, this is what I know of them. Here it is quite accepted.
One admits one's sodomy, and it is spoken of at table in the hotel.

GUSTAVE FLAUBERT

Mr. _____ is hereby elected a full member of the above society
with all its privileges. Members are warned to select brother members
[and] have full opportunities to meet each others friends and sailors.

CERTIFICATE OF MEMBERSHIP, PANSIES OF AMERICA, 1930

We were going into a world full of temptations. . . . we must report
any boy at once who tried to get into our bed, never go for a walk with a boy
from another house, never make friends with anyone more than a year and a half older
(eventually it would be younger), and above all, not "play with ourselves."

CYRIL CONNOLLY

The Tarts [gay boys] had an important function
to play in making school (what it was
advertised to be) a preparation for public life.
They were not like slaves, for their favors were
(nearly always) solicited, not compelled.

C. S. LEWIS

Mao [Tse Tung]'s sexual activity was not confined to women. The young males who served as his attendants were invariably handsome and strong and one of their responsibilities was to administer a nightly massage as an additional aid to sleep. Mao insisted that his groin be massaged, too, . . .

LI ZHISUI

The black gay girls in the Village gay bars of the fifties knew each other's names, but we seldom looked into each other's black eyes, lest we see our own aloneness and our blunted power mirrored in the pursuit of darkness.

AUDRE LORDE

We, the androgens of the world, have formed this responsible corporate body to demonstrate by our efforts that our physiological and psychological handicaps need be no deterrent in integrating 10% of the world's population toward the constructive social progress of mankind.

INTERNATIONAL BACHELORS FRATERNAL ORDER FOR PEACE
AND SOCIAL DIGNITY [BACHELORS ANONYMOUS], 1950

It was chic to be queer, rather as it was chic to know something about the twelve-tone scale and about Duchamps's *Nude Descending a Staircase*.

ALAN PRYCE-JONES

I know they say that Trujillo is a tyrant but, tell me, do they say that Trujillo is a homosexual?

RAFAEL TRUJILLO

Fifteen years ago, it was taken for granted all over Morocco that anybody slept with anybody. No holds barred.

PAUL BOWLES

As deadly as they were sublime,
the tubs, though heaven for a spell,
turned out to be a steaming hell:
so many men, so little time.

ROBERT BOUCHERON

It was not dirty sex as much as symbolic sex at the St. James, the sex of promise and fantasy where the players moved in prescribed patterns as in a religious pageant.

DOTSON RADER

If you think I'm an old spinster—think again.

LUDWIG WITTGENSTEIN

What a pity one can't now and then change sexes! I should love to be a dowager Countess.

LYTTON STRACHEY

It's no wonder we know how to dress: we've spent centuries in closets.

ISAAC MIZRAHI

CHAPTER THIRTEEN

PEOPLE
we
LOVE

It's absurd to divide people into good or bad.
People are either charming or tedious.

OSCAR WILDE

If Oscar Wilde were alive today
he'd be on every talk show.
He'd replace Suzanne Somers!

MICHAEL MUSTO

We have shown America that we are no longer afraid of ourselves.
We have had the courage in the face of an unprecedented onslaught to reach out
to each other and show the country the true meaning of family values.

DAVID GEFFEN

The real intent of my work is to reach the world at large,
to take the message of compassion and generosity
and understanding that I learned through the process of
being gay and sharing that with everyone.

ARMISTEAD MAUPIN

Queer
Notions
page 190

It's very important for us to remain visible, to not be the faceless, nameless citizens that we've been allowed to kind of be pushed back into over the years.

CANDACE GINGRICH

There are those who say that government shouldn't be involved in sexual issues. But when twelve million people a year are getting STDs, three million of them teenagers, I think somebody needs to get involved.

JOYCELYN ELDERS

Homosexuality is a problem because an unenlightened society has made it a problem, but I have received letters by the thousands (not just "occasionally") from gay people telling me that they wouldn't be straight if they had a choice.

ABIGAIL VAN BUREN

Homosexuality is not a crime. People have to realize that although you may be different, you must be treated in the same way as every other South African.

NELSON MANDELA

We have no concept of homosexuality as maladaptive.
That is a value judgement we do not make or feel, or find in our present work.

WILLIAM H. MASTERS AND VIRGINIA E. JOHNSON

*Homosexuality is not only
not immoral, but is moral in a
real and positive sense, and is good
and right and desirable.*

FRANK KAMENY

One should no more deplore homosexuality than left-handedness. . . .
Homosexual affection can be as selfless as heterosexual affection, and therefore
we cannot see that it is in some way morally worse.

THE RELIGIOUS SOCIETY OF FRIENDS (THE QUAKERS)

[Homosexuality] is nothing to be ashamed of, no vice,
no degradation, it cannot be classified as an illness. It is a great
injustice to persecute homosexualityas a crime, and a cruelty too.

SIGMUND FREUD

Homosexuals are allowed to emerge from the closet. . . . We have come a long way in recognizing that people are individually created, not stamped from a mold in the shape of a majority group.

Emily Post's Etiquette, 14th edition

It is a tragedy, I feel, that people of a different sexual type are caught in a world which shows so little understanding for homosexuals, is so crassly indifferent to the various gradations of gender and their great significance in life.

EMMA GOLDMAN

People may criticize the university for trying to be politically correct. But there's also a thing called trying to keep up with the world.

TEA SILVESTRE

Some of my most brilliant teachers and some of my classmates were gay. They were just part of the community of people. I think that is what is important to understand.

JESSE JACKSON

Without homosexuals there'd be no Hollywood.

ELIZABETH TAYLOR

Homosexuals can love, give, elevate others and elevate themselves. It's surely better to go to bed with a boy friend than to go traveling in Nazi Germany.

JEAN-PAUL SARTRE

There is probably no sensitive heterosexual alive who is not preoccupied
at one time or another with his latent homosexuality.

NORMAN MAILER

Gay men are guardians of the masculine impulse.
To have anonymous sex in a dark alleyway
is to pay homage to the dream of male freedom.
The unknown stranger is a wandering pagan god.
The altar, as in pre-history, is anywhere you kneel.

CAMILLE PAGLIA

There's nothing wrong with going to bed with somebody of your own sex—
they should draw the line at goats.

ELTON JOHN

All of my sexual experiences when I was young were with girls.
I mean, we didn't have those sleep over parties for nothing.

MADONNA

It's such a feat that I actually married someone who is heterosexual.

RICKI LAKE

When you see two women walking hand in hand, Just look 'em over and try to understand; . . .

BESSIE SMITH

Went out last night with a crowd of my friends, They must've been women, 'cause I don't like men. . . .

MA RAINEY

**I'm both black and gay.
As far as I'm concerned, I've hit the jackpot.**

JAMES BALDWIN

I loved Jimmy and so did he.

NINA SIMONE, ON JAMES BALDWIN

Martin Luther Queen.

DOROTHY DEAN, ON JAMES BALDWIN

I'm an alcoholic

I'm a drug addict

I'm a homosexual

I'm a genius

TRUMAN CAPOTE

I never wanted to be a woman, I wanted to be an actress. There's a difference to me.

CHARLES BUSCH

Davis, Bette (Ruth Elizabeth Davis, 1908–89) Member of the A-list of gay male icons, and staple part of the act of every drag queen in the galaxy, . . .

WILLIAM STEWART

PEOPLE
WE LOVE
page 197

CHAPTER FOURTEEN

PEOPLE
we
HATE

If homosexuality were the normal way, God would have made Adam and Bruce.

ANITA BRYANT

Freedom from homosexuality is possible through repentance and faith in Jesus Christ.

ANTHONY FALZARANO

This message is the only hope they have. We are talking about people going to hell. We've got to stop them.

FRED PHELPS

We are told in the Bible to love all people, including those who sin against the Lord. For this reason, I must have love in my heart toward homosexual and lesbian people.

PAT ROBERTSON

Queer
Notions

Now listen, you queer. Stop calling me a crypto-Nazi
or I'll sock you in your goddamn face.

WILLIAM F. BUCKLEY, TO GORE VIDAL

What difference does it make?
They're just a couple of fags.

LEE RADZIWILL

She's not your garden-variety lesbian. She's a militant-activist-mean lesbian,
working her whole career to advance the homosexual agenda.

JESSE HELMS, ON ROBERTA ACHTENBERG

Jesse Helms put forth an amendment to the existing National Endowment for the
Arts legislation: No funding to artists who depict sexual organs or excretory organs.
I think that's funny coming from a big dickhead who's full of shit.

ROB NASH

Every lesbian spear-chucker in this country
hopes I get defeated.

BOB DORNAN

Homosexuality is funny, provided it's on the telly; off the telly homosexuals are only fit for being punched up.

Phillip Adams

I don't think an admitted lesbian should be Attorney General of the state of New York.

GUY MOLINARI

Homosexuality is a sickness just as baby-rape or wanting to become head of General Motors.

ELDRIDGE CLEAVER

The homosexual must be entirely eliminated. . . . Just think . . . how a people can be broken in nerve and spirit when such a plague gets hold of it.

HEINRICH HIMMLER

We've got to consider . . . the rights of those who are not homosexual and who give up a great deal of their privacy when they go into the military.

SAM NUNN

CHAPTER FIFTEEN

The
NEXT
GENERATION

"We're gonna teach our adopted son that tolerance is a virtue."

In this day and age, isn't everyone gay?

GEORGE GENE GUSTINES

Stonewall is not just about yesterday; for us it must also be about tomorrow.

VIRGINIA APUZZO

If one homosexual in Altoona, Pennsylvania, will never have to
be invisible again, then I will have done my job.

HARVEY MILK

Dear Sir, I am the sort of homosexual
you disapprove of since I am still in the closet.
I am twelve years old.

FROM A LETTER RECEIVED BY EDMUND WHITE AFTER
THE PUBLICATION OF *THE JOY OF GAY SEX*

This is a society that devalues our sexuality. During our formative years everything possible
is done to stomp on our feelings, and then somehow we are
supposed to emerge, capable of handling responsible, adult sexual relationships.

KIKI MASON

Queer
Notions
page 206

I wasn't aware of my sexuality but I was quite feminine as a kid. The only way I knew that was because of what was said to me every day—some tosser shouting "anti-man" or "battyman" as I walked down the street. Nine years of that fucked me up.

DAVID MCALMONT

I don't understand how you cannot know you're gay. Everybody masturbates. Obviously, you think about something.

MATTHEW GARCIA

Most gay and lesbian teens don't have it as good as my characters do. I wanted to create something people could go see and imagine the world as it could be. To imagine life better can have a very powerful impact, political and otherwise.

MARIA MAGGENTI

Johnny can't read, write, or do math,
but he knows how to put on a condom.

N'Tanya Lee

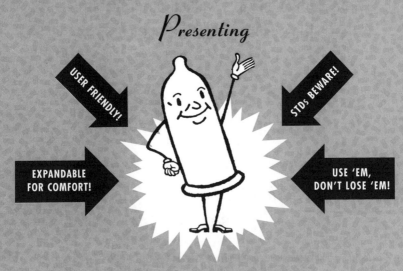

*If my children were struggling
with sexual orientation,
I would want to help them figure
out who they are and what they are
and how to be happy.*

RUDOLPH GIULIANI

! would tell my child that in the United States, adults are allowed to
do what they want to do in private so long as it doesn't hurt someone else.

ALAN DERSHOWITZ

Sure I have problems but they're not my fault. I can't help it;
I'm an adult child of heterosexuals.

TOD PATTERSON

**For many men, internalized homophobia is a form of
post-traumatic stress syndrome.**

RICK ISENSEE

THE **NEXT
GENERATION**

I imagine a world in which our genders had nothing to do with who we fall into bed with.

ARA WILSON

Some people know us as gay, some know us as straight. You leave college,
and suddenly people want to know what you are.
I can't classify it. All I know is that, right now, I'm in love with Jen.

KIM NAGY

I've kissed a girl; I've kissed a boy; so what's next?

JILL SOBULE

It's the job of the young to push the societal envelope.

JEANNE CORDOVA

The older ones became warped by propaganda.
We younger ones are mired in decadence.

WALLACE THURMAN

Queer
Notions

We are caught between the past that
formed us and a future we have yet to create.

VINITA SRIVASTAVA

The day we stop resisting our instincts, we'll have learned how to live.

FEDERICO GARCÍA LORCA

Perhaps the millenium will arrive, not with the elimination of
"gay fiction" sections from bookstores,
but with the establishment of "straight fiction" sections.

MARK MERLIS

Then, when the end of the world is at hand, the woman will not find
content with her husband, nor the man with his wife.

VYASA

Through a worldwide homophobic fog we are beginning to see, even dimly,
the outline of a global gay and lesbian reality. It is diverse and peculiar in every culture,
yet united at some deep, mysterious core of being. We are everywhere.

NANCY L. WILSON

For a long time now, gay men have remembered
to laugh at the idiosyncracies and campy
pleasures of gay culture; even lesbians (who have
occasionally been accused of humorousness)
are beginning to learn to chuckle.

MERYL COHN

You will never be rid of us, because we reproduce ourselves out of your bodies.

MARTHA SHELLEY

Later, in a more perfect society,
someone else just like me
is certain to appear and act freely.

CONSTANTINE CAVAFY

You may forget but
Let me tell you
this: someone in
some future time
will think of us

Sappho

Index of Names

About the Author

David Blanton is a political correspondent for The Gay Cable Network.
He appears regularly on the nationally televised program *Gay USA,* and has written for
The Village Voice and *POZ* magazine. He lives in New York City.